Jesus Unleashed My Potential

Steve Allmen
Laura Allmen

Published by: Matthew 25 29

Steven Daniel Allmen

1317 Edgewater Dr

STE 4737

ORLANDO, FL 32804

All illustrations and images are the property of Unleash Your Potential LLC

Content Editor: David Strauss

Interior & Cover Design: Barbara Wade

Author Coaching: David Strauss

ORDERING INFORMATION:

Special discounts are available on quantity purchases by corporations, associations, and organizations. Contact the publisher at the above address for special discounts.

Dedicated to our three children, Anthony, Olivia, and Jason, who have watched and are part of our journey. We are so happy and grateful for the gifts that you are and the time that we have been given. Our hope is that as you grow spiritually, Jesus will unleash your potential as well. We love you!

DISCLAIMER

This book is presented solely for educational and entertainment purposes only. The author and publisher are not offering it as a substitute for professional career, spiritual, or financial advice. It is not intended to replace a one-on-one relationship with a qualified spiritual, financial, or other similar professional advisor.

Neither the author nor the publisher shall be held liable or responsible to any person or entity with respect to any loss or incidents or consequential damages caused or alleged to have been caused, directly or indirectly, by the information contained herein.

Every person is different, and the suggested strategies contained herein may not be suitable for each unique situation.

TABLE OF CONTENTS

Book One
God is Always There
Laura Allmen

Introduction 9

The Struggle 17

Leap and Grow Your Wings 21

Mindset Matters 25

God Loves Goals 29

"Believe" 33

Words Have Power 35

God is in Control 41

Change is good 49

How Did We J.U.M.P.? 55

Allmen, Always, and Forever 61

Epilogue 65

Book Two
Navigating the Miracles
Steve Allmen

Introduction 71

Mindset is Everything 77

Happiness is a Choice 83

Words Are Powerful 93

Power of Words Exercise 105

Faith Over Fear 107

Reflect and Move Forward 109

Knowing–Doing Gap 119

Your Perception is Your Truth 123

Epilogue 129

JUMP INTRODUCTION

"On the other side of fear, there is freedom."

Have you ever wanted to make changes in your life but couldn't get past the feeling of being stuck—wondering if there is a way out?

Do you dream of a better life but are afraid to try something new because the uncertainty of the unknown overpowers your desire for improvement?

Have you lost your enthusiasm for life because you find yourself having to put your career responsibilities ahead of your family commitments and your relationship with God?

Maybe it's dissatisfaction with your health, your living environment, or your relationship with friends, family, or God. Only you know what it is, and it is big enough not to be ignored.

Perhaps, deep inside, you know there is more to life—more happiness, more adventure, more fulfillment, more abundance, more joy. You see it all around you. You yearn for more, but you don't know how or when to take that first step toward change.

If you were to look at your life right now as if it were a movie, and you don't like what you are seeing, what if you could change the direction of your life? What if there was a way out? Would you sneak a peek to see if it were safe, or would you take the risk, and dive in head-first and figure things out as you went along?

What if on the other side of fear there is freedom and opportunity? Would you pursue the opportunity or give in to your fear?

If you are looking for courage, permission, or a strategy to plan your escape and build your dream life, then get ready to jump into this book because it is going to share battle-tested insights that will give you the guts and faith to make your move.

How can we make such a bold statement? As faith-based Christians, believing in a living God, we discovered that no matter what you are going through, with applied faith, you can courageously walk through any challenge in your life and JUMP into the life of your choosing.

When we say JUMP, we don't mean it literally. JUMP, for us, is faith in action. You see, we all have the potential for greatness, but we have to make the decision and take the first step. God can't do that for us. But once we take that first step of faith, that is when God can unleash our potential.

This book is about taking that first step of faith—that JUMP, and discovering how God's miracle, Jesus, can unleash your potential.

Jesus Unleashed My Potential (J.U.M.P.)

Why are we so confident that this book will be your go-to solution for transforming your life? The reason is simple. Our life is a testimony of navigating through uncertainty by putting God first.

Ever since we were married, we have bounced around. Moving more than 16 times in our past 35 years of marriage, we know what it takes to let go and start over. From transitioning back to civilian life at the end of our short military career to relocating across the country seeking employment opportunities, we applied the same stop-and-go mindset each time we began our new life.

As a husband-and-wife team, instead of putting our ideas together in one book with one voice, we decided to write two short books in one. Even though we have been on this incredible journey together, we each have unique insights and experiences which we want to share from our individual perspectives.

We developed key insights into how to put God first as we managed change, embraced opportunity, and kept our relationship vibrant and alive. We share those key insights along with many of the challenges we faced and how we overcame them together. Finally, we share how we stepped out of the post-military, corporate world to work together and fulfill our future.

To simplify the sharing of our insights, we have broken them down into simple concepts that we will expand upon in each of our respective books.

LAURA'S INSIGHTS:
1. Leap and grow your wings
2. Mindset matters
3. God loves goals
4. "Believe"
5. Words have power
6. God is in control
7. Change is good

STEVE'S INSIGHTS:
1. Mindset is everything
2. Happiness is a choice
3. Words are powerful
4. Faith over fear
5. Reflect and move forward
6. Knowing-doing gap
7. Your perception is your truth

Each of the above are what we call foundational insights. They are the foundation upon which we have chosen to expand our hearts and mind, stay true to our relationship with God, and honor our commitment to learn and grow together.

Whether you are single or married, believe in God or not, or have a different spiritual path, each of our concepts stand on their own merits and apply to anyone's life.

As we share our story, you have two choices. You can read through this book quickly and grab whatever thoughts first jump out at you, or you can sip each page like a fine wine, think about and savor each message. Ideally you do both. Read it through once for overall insight and pleasure, and then read it for a second time to gather and absorb the key concepts. We recommend the latter because it will give you the greatest opportunity to expand your awareness.

This is not a just a read-and-put-down book. There are inspiration, humor, and tips on how to overcome your fear and step out in faith. Read each page with an open mind and the clear intention to make real and lasting improvements in your life.

We believe that God has guided our path to write this book. Let the journey get underway. We begin with Laura.

BOOK ONE

•————————————•

God Is Always There

LAURA ALLMEN

Laura's Introduction 9

The Struggle 17

Leap and Grow Your Wings 21

Mindset Matters 25

God Loves Goals 29

"Believe" 33

Words Have Power 35

God is in Control 41

Change is good 49

How Did We J.U.M.P.? 55

Allmen, Always, and Forever 61

Epilogue 65

INTRODUCTION

Have you ever wondered why some married couples live happily ever after and are still in love and still best friends after many years, while others are unhappily married and counting the days until they are no longer together?

While everyone has their unique circumstances, I'm going to share with you how my husband Steve and I have been able to stay together during the best of times and while things were falling apart, and how, after 36 years, we are still enthusiastic about life and each other.

Our success is because we learned how to J.U.M.P. Not literally, but as you read this book, the acronym will make sense. You will see that our spiritual journey defines our relationship. We are a work in progress—even to this day—always expanding our potential through our faith.

· · · · ·

Our journey begins with one simple question.

Does everything happen for a reason?

Regardless of how amazing or painful something may be, is there a bigger plan working in the background of our lives that we cannot see?

I ask this question because my life and my relationship with Steve have been a storybook tale of miracles, first disguised as missteps and challenges. Every difficulty guided us to hidden blessings. In fact, the title of this book came to me in a most unusual way.

We had the title determined before we ever started writing the book. Our original title was JUMP. However, we quickly discovered that many books had already been written using the title and we were asked to reconsider. While I was reflecting upon what the title could be, God delivered it to me while I was showering after a workout at our local gym. We have had many of these unusual strings of events that turned into blessings.

There is no doubt that I believe things happen for a reason, and it is a big part of why Steve and I have been together so long, through thick and thin.

Time has shown me that two powerful forces are working in our lives, and if we learn how to weave them together, our life will flow with grace and ease.

One is the power of God. The other is the power of our thoughts and beliefs, what many people call "mindset."

Everyone has a different idea of what God is, so for the purposes of this book, here is how I see God.

• • • • •

I believe in a living God with whom we can have an active relationship. A loving father who wants to partner with us and guide us to fulfil our purposes. He is God, the creator of the universe, and we are created in His image, which means that we also can create our own life. I believe God has a plan and purpose for our lives, but He also gives us free will to choose the things we do. He will adapt His plan according to our choices and the consequences of our mistakes, but He will never change His plan because He loves us. He has demonstrated that love through the death and resurrection of His Son, our Lord and Savior, Jesus Christ.

• • • • •

My understanding of God has evolved and matured over time through different events and experiences.

Our mindset is a collection of thoughts and beliefs that we have gathered over time through our experiences. They shape our view of life and form our daily habits. How we think, what we feel, and our choices will always match our mindset. Being aware of our mindset is a big deal because it also helps us understand our attitude toward life.

Like most people, I had a defining moment that shaped my life and beliefs. It occurred when I was 18.

When I was young, like most kids, I did not think my decisions all the way through, mostly because I didn't understand that every choice has its unique destiny. I also did not understand how God works in our lives. How could I? I did not even know who I was, let alone have the experience to gain a mature, spiritual perspective of life.

When we are kids, many of our decisions are based on impulse and wanting to be accepted by our friends. We aren't looking for our life partner, our career, or to solve the mysteries of life. We just want to have fun, be accepted, and learn what we can while in school.

The pressure to make lifelong choices builds while we are in high school. *Do I go to college? What do I want to do when I grow up?* Despite all the pressure, with rare exceptions, we're still too young to make long-term decisions.

Unbeknown to me, during my senior year of high school, I made a decision that would define my entire life.

It all started back in 1984 on our senior class trip. Back in the '80s, the seniors would take a trip to Daytona Beach for a week of "chaperoned" fun. I had never intended on going, but little did I know that God had a different plan. So, at the last minute, I decided to go.

We loaded up on the buses and headed to Daytona Beach. It was a week filled with parties and people—a hotel full of high school kids from all over. I remember the first time we met. I had come back from the downstairs club, and he was in our room. I'm not sure how we made the connection, but we did.

Unfortunately for him, I had my sights set on someone else. I had only gone on the trip to get a date for our senior prom. Unfortunately, I wasn't very popular, and it was crunch time.

He did ask me to dinner one night, and I politely declined. As the week came to a close, we exchanged numbers, and I knew that we would be going to prom. And I was right. We started dating shortly after we returned home.

It was a difficult relationship at first because my heart wasn't in it 100%, and looking back, I was a bit controlling. But our relationship progressed, and we were settling in. That was the summer of 1984.

I was scheduled to go away to college in the fall and attend Central Michigan University (CMU) in Mt. Pleasant, MI. This was based on Steve's decision to attend this college in the fall as well. But for some reason, possibly finances, Steve did not attend CMU. I was going alone. No friends were going, and my boyfriend backed out. I moved on campus in the dorms and roomed with three other girls that I had never met.

I would soon realize that we had nothing in common, and due to my lack of social skills, I would travel home 2.5 hours every weekend to my comfort zone and my boyfriend. This continued the entire semester, and I decided that living away from home was not my thing. I left "Mt. Unpleasant," as I called it, and moved back home.

Knowing what I know now, the term I was using for my location, "Mt. Unpleasant," was exactly what showed up—an unpleasant experience. Our words really do create our world. In January of 1985, I started taking classes at the local community college and got a job. By the spring of 1985, we were both going to community college and working.

School was not going well for Steve, and he decided to talk to a recruiter. I remember the day he went. His mother and I both said, *"Now, don't do something stupid and sign up."* He assured us both he was just going to talk to them. Many hours went by, and when he came home, he informed us that he had joined the Army for three years. He would be leaving in August.

When he left, I knew the Army would either make us or break us. As it turned out, I realized what I had found in Steve. The adage "you don't know what you've got until it is gone" was my truth.

I missed him tremendously. I wrote him every day and sometimes twice a day. I poured out my heart in those letters, missing him, motivating him, and encouraging him to make it through. I waited anxiously to receive a letter back, but I wasn't getting any. That's when I took matters into my own hands. I figured out a way to contact his drill sergeant.

Yes, you read that right. I called his drill sergeant and explained that my boyfriend wasn't writing me back. I don't remember the conversation, but I did start getting a weekly letter. He had made it through basic training at Fort Leonard Wood, Missouri, which was an amazing accomplishment since, prior to enlisting, he could not run a mile or do more than five pushups.

My dad, who was a tremendous father and friend, drove me some 12 hours to see Steve graduate from basic training. On the way, I was worried that I wouldn't like this new Steve. My dad reassured me that it would be fine. He was always a "glass half full" kind of guy, and he was right.

I was amazed when I saw this young man transformed. He had lost a lot of weight and was pretty much bald, but something had shifted in him. He was confident and had a plan. In my opinion, the military was pivotal in making Steve the amazing man he is today. Even though I hated the separation, rules, and the distance between us at the time, everything worked out. We watched Steve graduate, and the weekend was over before it began.

Steve was sent to Virginia for cooking school, and I went back home with my dad. After eight weeks, Steve finished school and was stationed at Ft. Stewart, Georgia. I flew down in February to see him and told him that *"I was not coming down for nothing."* He understood my innuendo and asked me to marry him that weekend.

Of course, not in the way I had expected.

When I arrived, he picked me up in a Jeep borrowed from his friend, and we drove to the beach just in time for the sunset. Perfect place for a proposal, right? Well, Steve knew I was expecting it, so he let the moment pass, wanting to surprise me. Later that weekend, in our hotel room, he asked me if I would be his forever. Obviously, I said "yes," although this was not the romantic proposal I had in my head. I now see that it is not how or where the proposal takes place; it's the people and the decision that matter most. Little did I know that he had asked my dad's permission at Christmas time.

We were married in September of 1986 and moved to Hinesville, GA, where he was stationed. Then, within a few months, he received orders to go to Korea, even though he was promised stateside duty. That's the good old government for you. I wrote letters to commanders, officers, congressmen, and anyone that I thought would help me keep Steve stateside, but to no avail. His orders to Korea stood.

We had only been married for nine months when he left. It seemed that we had just started this marriage thing, and now I had to live back at home with Mom and Dad. Not particularly fun if you've ever moved out on your own and had to move back. Little did I know that this was just the beginning of our many moves.

So, back to Michigan for me to live with Mom and Dad again— Pusan, Korea for him. Yet after a few months at home, I decided that I would go to Korea.

For one thing, our phone bills were $500-$600 per month, and this was on the "wall" phone (you know, the one that hangs on the wall; there were no cell phones yet). And secondly, we were newly married, and long-distance was not working out for us. I told Steve to find a place for us to live because I was going there. I even told him the precise month I would be arriving. It would be September.

Little did I know back then, at the young age of 20, that when you make a decision, things start to move in the direction of that decision to make it happen.

I arrived in Korea in September 1987 to celebrate our one-year anniversary. My decision to date and later marry Steve and then my decision to move to Korea set in motion a string of life experiences that would guide me to discovering seven insights that expanded my relationship with God, my husband, and my dreams and goals.

1. Leap and grow your wings
2. Mindset matters
3. God loves goals
4. "Believe"
5. Words have power
6. God is in control
7. Change is good

Each of these insights comes with a lot of struggle, personal growth, and renewed faith to believe and trust in God.

THE STRUGGLE

"Today's tears water tomorrow's gardens."
— *Matshona Dhliwayo*

It wasn't always easy. We had many fights during the first year. Mostly due to my loneliness, lack of friends, isolation, and boredom. Steve worked long hours and had a routine for using his time—working, then hanging out with the guys after to play basketball. We only had one car, and he had it at work. So, there I sat at home with not much to do. And if I thought Georgia was hard, Korea would prove to be harder.

Steve had been in Korea for about three months without me. The many phone calls and arguments over the phone were taking a toll, and I knew I had to join him there. I set a date and started working another job to earn money. After about three months, the day had finally arrived.

I remember the outfit I was wearing and the huge tearful goodbye to my parents—tears of sadness, the unknown, and joy all wrapped together. I was a 20-year-old girl leaving the country for the first time and flying alone. When I finally arrived after over 15 hours of travel, I was less than happy to see him. Here's why.

I had traveled from Detroit to Alaska to Korea. When I arrived at the airport, hundreds of Korean people were waiting for their family or friends to arrive. Airports in the 1980s were nothing like they are today. You could be waiting at the gate for people to depart or arrive. As I walked into the airport, a woman held a sign that spelled my last name ALLMEN. Steve was nowhere to be found. I approached the women and somehow figured out that Steve was not there. I didn't know Korean, and they didn't speak much English. I was hustled to the Northwest airlines offices and observed people talking and making phone calls.

I learned that Steve's flight to Seoul, where I was, had been canceled due to inclement weather. So now the airline would put me up in a hotel because of the late hour. The airport was closing for the day as it was about 11:00 p.m., and there were only a few people there. I was afraid, tired, hungry, and did not know what to expect. I was taken to a small green Hyundai (a popular car in Korea) with my suitcase and instructed to get in. We drove wildly through the streets and ended up at a hotel. I got out and went in. No one spoke English. I was given a room, but my suitcase had to stay out—no explanation why.

There was a refrigerator in the room, and I opened it, hoping there was something to eat. There was! Dry fish and other things I did not recognize. Since I am allergic to fish, that was a no. So, I went to the front desk and asked to use the phone. I tried to explain that I wanted to call the U.S. and the man helped me call home. My parents were *frantic*. I recall my dad asking me where I was and as I cried, I said, "I don't know. It's all in Korean." Not sure what I was hoping to accomplish at that point. I mean, what could my parents do from across the world? Maybe I just needed to hear a familiar voice to calm my fears.

That night was a long one for sure. I woke up early, and a man knocked on my door to instruct me to get in the car again. I followed his instructions and was taken to the airport. I boarded a plane that would arrive in Pusan about an hour later. When I saw Steve, I was not happy. How could he leave me in a foreign country to fend for myself overnight? He did have his valid reasons, but that would not make me feel any better that day.

When I arrived, I learned that there was not much to do in Korea when in the military. One thing everyone did to pass the time was drink. I realized that Steve had gotten pulled into the drinking scene and had become a borderline alcoholic.

Timing is everything. And my arrival changed Steve's habits. After our initial bumps and bruises, we once again settled into our marriage. Things were coming together for a time until we aligned ourselves with the wrong people, and by doing so, our relationship began to unravel. I knew that I needed to leave Korea ASAP. Steve was about three months away from leaving Korea, but I would not leave with him. So, I left by myself to move back home again. When he arrived back in Michigan, things cleared up, and we spent our 30 days of leave connecting with friends and family.

We could have easily given up and thrown in the towel. If ever we were close to divorce, it was then. We choose to work on the things that were wrong and make them better. I have learned that love is a choice. It's not just a feeling of butterflies and kisses. It's a choice to love when it's hard—to get over feelings that come and go and just make it work. So many people today always think the grass is greener on the other side. They don't realize that you can make your grass green if you water it. So that's what we have been doing over the years—choosing each other and watering our grass.

Over the years, we did have different struggles. We had to learn how to parent together and raise our kids. We had to learn how to handle holiday celebrations to include both sides of the family. Many times, we didn't agree and would argue. I was a stubborn one, and, at times, I would be silent for days. Someone reading this right now knows what I mean. It's not an effective way to handle disagreements in a relationship, and thankfully after many years, I did correct this problem.

In retrospect, it was quite a rough road for us. There we days and weeks when I would look at Steve and think, "this is who I married?" Those are phases that many marriages go through, and if we can just hold on and work through it, it will work out. I think many people just give up too quickly.

So, my advice is, "Hang in there with all your might." Your family is worth it.

I want to be clear that I am in no way recommending this if there is abuse of any kind. That would require professional advice, which is not my area of expertise. I am speaking from my own experience in hopes of helping others.

1st Lesson

LEAP AND GROW YOUR WINGS

• • •

We must walk consciously only part way toward our
goal, and then leap in the dark to our success.
— Henry David Thoreau

We are not a typical story of how to succeed in marriage. I mean, we were very young. Steve was 19, and I had just turned 20. We jumped into marriage without ever talking about what we wanted or expected of each other and our marriage. We never asked the important questions like:

Do we want children? If so, how many? Will I work or stay home with the kids? Church? Will we go? If so, to what church? Who's handling the finances? What will the holidays look like? Pets? Location? Where will we settle down?

I am incredibly blessed to be sitting here, 36 years later, happily married, and now setting goals with my husband for our future. How did this happen? Well, God had us meet different people that would change the trajectory of our lives.

Let's go back a few years. My husband was thriving in corporate America. He was at the height of his career, and the income was amazing! We had waited years for this to happen, and here we were. Steve's hard work and determination had finally paid off.

As I look back, though, I can remember times when he received outrageous bonuses, and I couldn't, or should I say, wasn't happy. Because although the money was amazing, my health was not. I struggled for about 25 years with bladder problems, and that's a book in and of itself.

I remember standing in the kitchen next to the coffee pot with my back turned to my husband. He was so excited and proud of this particular bonus, and so was I, yet tears were flowing down my face because I had the belief that no amount of money would make me feel less pain—and I was in constant pain. But that night, we knelt together and thanked God for this extraordinary blessing.

My point is that, at the time, even a big bonus would not make me feel better. Yes, it helped and is always a blessing, but money cannot make your health return. Sure, you can get the material things and pay bills, but it can't make you healthy, and I wanted that more than anything.

Within the next few years, the upper management changed numerous times. Our bonuses became less and less until finally, they were non-existent. Now, my husband's salary was less than he was making ten years prior, and there was no hope in sight. He knew things were not changing when they walked his boss of 16 years out and fired him. We had been through this two other times, and this time would be no different.

I learned that the automotive industry is good when it's good, but when it's bad, it's bad. This time we had reason to believe he would be promoted because, for over a year, that was the word both Steve and his boss were getting from upper management. But it did not turn out that way. Sadly, they hired someone from outside and expected my husband to train his replacement.

He was not going to be in that position this time, and that's when he decided to JUMP! He asked to get the same deal as his boss, a six-month severance package, and to our surprise, it was denied.

We were with this company for over 16 years. Steve and his team had brought it to the top, and even built a brand-new world-class building from the ground up—and nothing, no severance. To say we were disappointed was an understatement.

As the wife, I've got to tell you, I was scared. That meant no benefits. No medical, dental, vision—nothing. How would this all pan out? I didn't know. But I did trust my husband and knew that God always had our back.

Trusting God does not make it easy, but it does make it possible. So here we are in our 50s, about to do something unheard of.

Do we just do it? Do we leave what we have been brought up to believe: "Get a good job and retire at 70?"

At this point, Steve made the decision. He was done with corporate America, and I couldn't blame him. But what would he do?

Was he walking away to work with me?

That was crazy because I was making about $300 a month.

It was time to leap and grow our wings. We had a faith mindset, so we leapt, knowing that God was our wings.

Those benefits that I was worried about—God took care of that almost immediately. I recently joined a referral group to get my business growing and meet new people. A woman in the group helped self-employed people like us get insurance.

And that's how God works. That day we had medical benefits! We took this as confirmation that we made the right career decision and only had to continue moving forward with faith.

MINDSET MATTERS

• • •

*"Once your mindset changes, everything on the outside
will change along with it."*
— Steve Maraboli, *Life, the Truth, and Being Free*

I was 54 years old before I was introduced to the word "mindset." It's a commonly used term but what does it mean? What is a "mindset"?

Very simply, it is your view and approach to life—based on your thoughts, beliefs, attitude, assumptions, and expectations.

Your mindset is a collection of thoughts and beliefs that you have gathered over time through your experiences. They shape your view of life and form your daily habits. How you think, what you feel, and your choices will always match your mindset.

Mindset is all-encompassing, affecting every aspect of your life. Most people are not aware of their overall mindset unless it is brought to their attention by another person or by a sudden disruption to their life. Here are a few examples of different mindsets.

FAITH-BASED MINDSET

You are willing to make decisions even if there is no evidence to support the possibility of the outcome you desire, based on a belief in God.

VICTIM MINDSET

You live in the past and have negative expectations for life. Overall, you believe or expect that, ultimately, people will harm you.

WINNER MINDSET

You have positive expectations. You orient your mind toward self-improvement, have self-discipline, and are willing to do the work to achieve your ambitions.

LOSER MINDSET

This is tied to low self-esteem. You don't give your best effort because you see yourself as a failure or not good enough. You give up before you even try.

LEADERSHIP MINDSET

You believe that everyone has hidden strength and potential, and you have the patience and drive to bring out the best in others.

HEALTH-CONSCIOUS MINDSET

You make food and lifestyle decisions based on what is best for your overall health and well-being.

Without defining them, here are a few more:

- Mother's mindset
- Golf mindset
- Artist mindset
- Spiritual mindset
- Athletes' mindset

These are just a few examples of mindset. As you can see, each mindset is based on a set of beliefs and expectations and where you are placing your focus and attention.

Your mindset matters. If you have a victim's mindset, it will be difficult to be happy because you are expecting to be harmed. If you have a loser's mindset, you will avoid situations where you may fail. If you have a winner mindset, you will put yourself in situations that challenge you.

For most people, their mindset is a habit. Every day they make decisions using the same level of thinking that got them to where they are now, and most of us do this unconsciously.

If you want to achieve something new or different in life or raise your standards, you have to develop a mindset that matches the results you want to achieve. It's not easy, but the way you do it is by surrounding yourself with people who have the results you want so that you learn their habits and how they think and make decisions. If you are anything like I was, I wasn't surrounded by those people. Yes, I had friends that were doing well, but not necessarily better than me, and that's what I needed—to be around people that were where I wanted to be.

How did I discover the importance of mindset?

One day I asked my chiropractor about some pain in my shoulder. He said he had the fix. I assumed that he would adjust me and that would take care of it. He made the adjustment, but it wasn't the solution he was recommending. Instead, it was a product that could help with inflammation. So, I said, sign me up! I decided right there. I didn't ask how much it would cost. I just bought the product right away.

Why would I do this? Well, over the last 8 years or so, my family had formed a relationship with the doctor, and we trusted his opinion. He had tried the product on himself and had amazing results, so why not give it a try for my situation? Too many times we overthink before making decisions. Not this time; I would just jump right in.

Did I just sign up in a Multi-level Marketing (MLM)company? Yep, that's what I did.

I had always been a student of health and wellness, and this made sense. Decision made!

I called my husband on my way home and told him I bought a new product that would help with inflammation and our overall health. And, by the way, I don't know how much it cost or how it really works and, oh yeah, I joined a business so I can share it with others. Steve didn't blink an eye. He just went with it and soon we were all taking the product.

This new business opportunity opened the floodgates for us. That decision was the tip of the iceberg for my transformation. It was a decision that would lead my husband and me to attend a conference in Austin, Texas, the following year. Initially, I didn't want to go, but a nice vacation seemed fun. So, I asked my husband to go, and he said he would come but not go to the conference, just enjoy the day at the pool. That was good enough for me.

As it turned out, we both attended, and the conference opened doors for us that we did not even know existed. But, most importantly, we would learn the power of written goals. When I say power, I mean we discovered that God loves goals.

GOD LOVES GOALS

• • •

Know what you want. Clarity is Power.
And vague goals promote vague results.
— Robin Sharma

Looking back on my life, I realize that I was unconsciously setting goals like, I'm going to live in Korea with my husband and have children, but I never really sat down and made written goals.

God loves written goals because when you write them down, you are making a declaration to yourself and God that this is where you are placing your focus and attention, and you are willing to work through all the wins, losses, obstacles, setbacks, and victories. This, I found out, is also written in the Bible in Habakkuk 2:2, where it says:

"Then the Lord said to me, Write down this vision clearly. Inscribe it on tablets so one may easily read it."

Clarity is power. God cannot work in your life if you are unfocused or wishy-washy. For 54 years, I just drifted along, doing well, but never really having any clearly defined goals for myself. That changed when I immersed myself in *Thinking into Results*. It's an amazing program that opened my eyes to the power of my thoughts and my words.

Fast forward to the conference. It was 2019—a few years before the pandemic. We found ourselves in a room filled with happy, motivated people, all wanting to help each other and be healthy. Now, these were my people. I remember hearing someone speak, and she said something like: "Maybe God has led you here today, and this is for you."

I knew right there that this was something I wanted to do. It was what I would call a defining moment.

At this conference, I met a gentleman by the name of Dr. Kenny Harless, who studied under the great Bob Proctor. Dr. Harless would become my mentor, and, through his workshop, *Thinking into Results,* I learned about mindset and paradigms (beliefs we hold). I learned to picture what I do want and not what I don›t want. Soon enough, doors would open for me that no one could ever imagine, including the healing of my diseased bladder that affected my health for many years.

My health issues started back in my 20s. I was diagnosed with interstitial cystitis, a painful bladder condition. Not only that, but shortly after my first son was born, I began to have urinary retention.

That was years of doctor appointments, medications, urodynamic testing, and in the end, learning how to catheterize myself to empty my bladder. I did this for several years—even through my second pregnancy. But I did have a determination to find an answer. I learned that you should always get a second opinion, and I also learned to never give up.

I found a brilliant doctor that did all the tests yet another time and found that I had an obstruction in the neck of my bladder. It was very rare, and it required surgery. At the time, I had three children, with the youngest being 2. The recovery was difficult, but thankfully, I made it through with the help of family and friends. The surgery was successful! We also discovered that the cystitis was probably a misdiagnosis.

For this reason, I have learned to always get a second opinion. I took medication that had side effects for over seven years for a condition I did not have. My bladder functioned well after the surgery for about 8 years. Then one day, actually New Year's Eve, I felt an awful full feeling and couldn't empty my bladder. So, to the hospital I went, and they had to catheterize me, and the struggle began again.

I can't remember all the details, but I had another surgery with another doctor because mine had retired. The surgery never really worked, so I was back to cathing again. I was devasted. It affected my mental well-being. But I persevered through the pain and the cathing. I tried every new therapy you could think of. And like I said, I am determined like that. The end diagnosis was unexplained urinary retention. "Just keep cathing," they said. Well, that was not an option for me.

As part of the *Thinking into Results* program, I had to develop a goal and write it on a goal card.

This was new!

Who does this kind of thing?

Well, most successful people have written goals. Who knew? But as I started to become more aware, I began seeing lots of people doing the same thing.

Steve Harvey has written goals and vision boards.

Jim Carey wrote himself a check for $10,000,000 for acting services. He dated it and put it in his wallet, and by that date, on the check, he received the exact amount: $10,000,000.

It was eye-opening to me, and now I see it everywhere. It's like when you buy a new grey Jeep, and you suddenly start seeing grey Jeeps everywhere.

I wrote down a few important goals, but the most significant was my goal for my bladder, which went like this: "I am so happy and grateful now that my bladder is functioning properly and is pain-free."

I wrote this goal down every day from February till December. In December of that year, my bladder was functioning properly and pain-free. Finally, about a year and a half later, in November of 2021, I got rid of all catheters and supplies. Doctors had told me my condition would be forever, but there I was with a pain-free bladder that was emptying without using a catheter.

It wasn't an instant miracle, although God does those too. It was what happens when you have a faith mindset. I did my part, and that allowed God to do His part. All things are possible when you believe.

In fact, the bible says it in Mark 11:24: "Therefore, I tell you whatever you ask for in prayer, believe that you have received it, and it will be yours."

I had prayed and prayed, but it was the belief part that I struggled with. At first, I couldn't wrap my head around this thinking into results, but I watched as people in the group started changing things in their life, and it gave me the belief to change mine, too. And it worked!

As I discovered, God loves goals. My belief was not just in the healing, but that God was the source of my healing.

I believe God puts people in our path at the right time for the right reason, and if we are open to receiving the timely message, good things will follow.

4th Lesson

"BELIEVE"

• • •

Faith does not make things easy. It makes them possible.
— Luke 1:37

Let me tell you about the word "believe."

This past summer, I struggled and wondered if what we were doing was right. So, let's be real: my husband was leaving a six-figure income.

Was it all going to work out?

I am a believer, but like everyone else, I'm human, and sometimes my flesh kicks in and makes me doubt. Trust me—I'm working on that. Anyway, I was up north having a conversation with a cousin of mine that I only see maybe once a year when we make the trip to Port Austin, Michigan— a place we went to as kids. It was a beautiful conversation—one of my most memorable for sure.

When he woke up in the morning, my cousin Roger told me that Ciocia Honey (my granny) had come to him in a dream and wanted him to say to me to "remember the spoon." He was hesitant to tell me, but he did, and I stood there looking at him dumbfounded. I didn't know anything about a spoon. He assured me it would come to me, and we parted ways.

It was a three-hour drive home, so I asked my mom, who was traveling with me, if she remembered anything about granny and a spoon? She said no, she didn't recall a conversation about that.

A few weeks later, I called my sister Lisa and asked her if she knew anything about granny and a spoon, and she said excitedly, "YES, you don't?"

I was shocked! What do you know? I asked. She said, "I have the wooden spoons." I said, what wooden spoons? She took a picture of the spoons and texted them to me. What my granny had done was she had written the word "believe" on a wooden spoon. It was spelled wrong because granny only had a 3rd-grade education and was going blind when she wrote it. My sister was there and said she wanted the spoon, but my mom said, "no, she spelled it wrong. So, my mom wrote the word "believe" correctly on another spoon.

My sister has in her possession two wooden spoons with the word "believe" written on them. Sometimes God uses people to let us know we are on the right path, and he did that with my cousin Roger and another day with my sister Lisa.

"BELIEVE" is a powerful word.

Some months later, the doubt crept back in, and we questioned. Were we spiritually on the right path? My husband prayed that morning that God would help me know that we are. Within the hour, I got a text from my cousin. He was walking his dog, and the dog stopped. The dog never stops, so when he did, he looked down and saw a rock with the word believe written on it. He felt he had to text me to say, "You're on the right spiritual journey."

WOW, that's all I can say. God is so good. He speaks when we need to hear it in ways that we can't even imagine, and He does answer prayers.

One more time, I would slip into doubt mode because what I've learned is we have many paradigms about how life is supposed to go, and not having a "normal" job was a whole new way of life for me. Feeling insecure and doubting yet again, I went to the mailbox, and there was a big envelope with my name on it. So, I excitedly opened it to find a small bracelet with "believe" on it.

I had ordered the bracelet weeks before and had forgotten, but at the right time, the package came to remind me again to BELIEVE that all things were working out.

WORDS HAVE POWER

• • •

You can change your world by changing your words.
Remember, death and life are in the power
of the tongue.
— Joel Osteen

Our words have power.

Did you ever say something you didn't mean? I know I have! I've also spoken words without understanding their power. Until recently, I didn't believe or understand their power. Boy, have my eyes been open to the power they have. I look back and see times when I spoke words that have come to pass. So let me share what I mean.

When my husband was deployed to Korea, nine months after we were married, I was furious because housing options on the military base were only available to soldiers with a higher rank. For me, that was completely unacceptable.

I said these words to him: "Find me a place; I'm coming to live there."

It was a bold statement for a young, newly married 20-year-old. I'm not sure what he thought, but this I know: he found me a place to live, and within four months, I arrived in Korea. It was honestly as simple as that. I said the words, and it came to pass.

Another example of the power of words happened recently, which is sad because I now know their power. But I'm human and still learning and growing and trying to get this thing called life, right.

We had just sold my dream house and moved into an apartment. Since we had never really lived in an apartment and were coming from a newly built house, I had expectations of how things would be. Because of the housing market, we had to sign the lease sight unseen. Yes, that's right, we did not see it before we had the keys—not something I would recommend.

Well, we had to fill out a form and list all the things that were not right or broken. We even took photos of some of the things we thought were more of a priority. Then I called the property manager to tell them that the pavers in the back were broken and needed to be fixed because they were a trip hazard. I had dogs and an older mother that could trip and fall.

Fast forward to the second time my mom came over to visit us in our new apartment. She decided it was good to go out and have a cigarette. We set up a bucket with sand in it for her to put out her smokes and placed the bucket to the end of the pavers. Because our apartment had no gutters, if the bucket were close to the house, it would fill with water. Hence, we moved it to the end of the pavers.

The doorbell rang. The grandbaby was sleeping. Dogs started to bark, and as I tried to manage all of the commotion, I lost sight of dear old mom. As I looked out the slider, she was on her knees at the end of the pavers. I thought maybe she had dropped something, but I knew she had tripped on those pavers when she didn't move.

I rushed out to find her bewildered and bleeding. She had hit her face on the bricks and was bleeding from her mouth. We got her up to her feet to see the damage, and it was clear her lip was split, and her top tooth was coming out. She was checked out at the hospital, and there was no major damage other than two stitches in her upper lip and a tooth that came out, root and all.

A few months later, I realized I had said, "Those pavers are a trip hazard, and my mom could fall." Wow! Got to learn to zip the lip and watch the words.

In my search for the power of words, I found many people that speak about it. People like Joel Osteen, Steve Harvey, and Bob Proctor, to name a few. Joel Osteen tells a story of a classmate who kept saying, "When I am old, I will be bald and fat." Joel ran into him years later, and he was bald and fat! He kept telling himself that repeatedly, and he got exactly what he said.

Steve Harvey has said that when people say, "I'll never be rich," it's a sure thing they won›t. Steve has a great testimony. He tells of a day in 6th grade when the teacher asked the children to write down what they wanted to be on a piece of paper. She then called them to the front of the class to share the answer. Then, when Steve Harvey went to the front of the class, she asked him what he wanted to be? Steve, who had a stuttering problem at the time, simply said, «I want to be on television.»

The teacher said, "Do you know anyone on television, Steve?"

He said, "No,"

She asked, "Is anyone in your family on television?"

"No."

She continued, "What makes you think you're going to be on television?" She thought he did not take the assignment seriously and called his parents.

That day, he left school dejected, knowing he would get in trouble when he got home. When he finally got home, his parents were arguing. His mom was mad at what he wrote down, but his father was not. Before he went to sleep, his father told Steve to put that paper in his drawer and read it every morning and every night. So, he did, and guess what? Steve Harvey is on TV every day. Our words create our world, so why not create the world we want?

I'm not saying that this can be done overnight. It takes time and discipline, and a willingness to change. But it is possible.

Many times, in my youth, I would pray but not know God's word or how to speak it. But, as I've grown spiritually, I know the power of God's words and His promises. I've seen God move mountains and change destinies. When my kids were in high school, I started posting positive affirmations and bible verses where we would see them daily, places like the shower, the mirror, the door, inside their lunch, the car, and sometimes under their pillow before bed. I learned that when we get God's word in us, we can use them and speak to them when we need them. Not only God's word but the truth of who we are.

I believe God wants us to be happy, abundant, prosperous, loving, and successful in all we do. But many times, our thoughts and words hold us back from those blessings. There are also times when the words others speak over us or about us hold us back. I noticed a few things holding my kids back, and I wanted to help, so up went the affirmations all over the shower wall.

You have a captive audience in the shower, so why not? I noticed my son struggling with being happy, so I made an affirmation that said, "I AM HAPPY." He struggled with his workouts in gym class, so "I AM STRONG," with a picture of weights went up.

I noticed my daughter struggling with her looks, so "I AM BEAU-TIFUL" and "I AM FEARFULLY AND WONDERFULLY MADE" went up.

Whatever the problem, I had a positive affirmation or scripture to solve it. A new thought said repeatedly over time will help anchor that new thought in your mind, so why not try it on my kids and me.

Some of my favorite affirmations are bible verses; words from God to speak over my life. Below are a few of my favorites.

Jeremiah 29:11 "For I know the plans I have for you declares the Lord, plans to prosper you and not harm you, plans to give you a hope and a future."

This one, I pray often when things aren't going the way I've planned.

Joshua 1:9 "This is my command-Be strong and courageous! Do not be afraid or discouraged. For the Lord, your God is with you wherever you go."

This speaks to circumstances that may cause fear.

Mark 11:24 "Therefore I say to you, whatever things you ask when you pray, believe that you receive them, and you will have them."

It is in the belief that we receive, and sometimes, in fact, most times, it is hard to wrap our heads around things we are believing for.

James 4:2 "You have not because you ask not."

This clearly speaks to the "ask." God cannot give you something unless you ask for it. And sometimes, you will get what you ask for but not in the way you were thinking. God's ways are so much higher than ours.

Isaiah 54:17 "No weapon formed against you will prosper."

I love this verse when faced with something coming against me.

Isaiah 53:5 "But He was wounded for our transgressions, He was bruised for our iniquities: The chastisement for our peace was upon Him, And by His stripes, we are healed."

I rely on this verse always. I believe that Jesus is our healer and that in His name, people are healed today. For any sickness or healing, I pray.

John 16:33 "I have told you these things so that you may have peace in me. In this world, you will have trouble. But take heart! I have overcome the world."

This verse gives me hope in all my circumstances and trials because I know that Jesus has overcome the world and He is with me.

6th Lesson

GOD IS IN CONTROL

• • •

"Keep trusting God...He is always in control even when
your circumstances may seem out of control."
— *Unknown*

Looking back, I can now see all the times that God has made everything work out for my good. One example would be the timing of my children. I wanted to have four children, one after the other. That was not to be my story. I had a miscarriage first, and then within a year, I had my first son. That's a whole story in and of itself.

In 1989 I struggled with secondary infertility for six years. It was another difficult time for us. We had two prior pregnancies. One ending is a miscarriage and the other nearly killed my son and me due to delivery issues and an accidental cut in my uterus. Not being able to get pregnant was something I didn't understand.

I had never heard of "secondary infertility," as the doctors called it. We went through all the testing except a laparoscopy—something I just didn't want to do because it involved surgery. Still, after six years of trying to conceive, without success, I decided to do the procedure. They found nothing that would explain infertility, but, to our surprise, I was pregnant with our daughter the next month. She was born in November 1995. My second son came without any difficulty at all and was, in fact, a pleasant surprise in April of 1999.

What I know is that I would have been a crazy momma with three kids close in age. What the timing did was allow me to enjoy each one separately. When my daughter was born, my oldest son was in kindergarten, which gave me the entire morning with my daughter. When the third child came, my daughter was in pre-kindergarten, which allowed me mornings with my baby.

It all worked out perfectly according to God's plan. Was it easy? No. The struggles, doubts, and stress of trying to get pregnant for six years were rough, but we made it through. One thing I know that we did was pray together every day. For us, it was a Catholic prayer to St. Jude, the patron saint of hopeless cases. It was all we knew at the time, and I believe God answered our recited prayer.

Now I can look back and say, "Thank you, God, for doing it your way and not mine." Sometimes when we are in it, we think we have a good plan. However, when you look back, you can connect the dots and see that God›s plans are always better.

The timing of my children was not the only thing that I can look back on and see that God was in control. Maybe you're a lot like I was. Going through life raising a family caught up in the chaos of every-day life and not seeing God's hand in it. But what I've learned is God is always working even when we don't see or feel it. If you can relate to this or are struggling in any way, I would encourage you to listen to the song "Way Maker" by Leland and simply soak in the lyrics.

This brings me to another example of God being in control—my short-lived but highly rewarding career. After one of our last moves, I reconnected with a longtime childhood friend, Amy. We decided to become nurse aides. I was about 40 years old at the time and hadn't gone to school in some years. But with a friend doing it, I mustered up enough confidence to go. We successfully passed the exam and became nurse aides at a hospice center in Michigan.

I knew after a few weeks that this was my calling for the moment. I was never scared, apprehensive, or nervous—it was easy for me. I loved being able to help people at the end of their lives feel comfortable and peaceful, and I loved interacting with and caring for the family members that were struggling with their grief.

My mom was a nurse, and I thought about being a nurse when I was little, but then life happened, kids happened, and I got lost in the shuffle. But being a nurse aide was very fulfilling for me. After hospice, I moved on to nursing homes/rehab, where I would get to love the elderly and motivate people to get better and go home.

Somehow, I went from death to life, and in my heart, I decided that hospice was a season I would not go back to. I loved hearing their stories and memories. Just making them feel happy brought me much joy. I only worked part-time, but the days were long. Working in that career, I saw first-hand the many problems in this end-of-life care system—a system that has spiraled downhill.

As time went by, the place where I worked was constantly changing directors, and with each change, the facility got worse. We were short-staffed, overworked, and taken advantage of, and the patients were suffering. So, I took it upon myself to speak to management, administrators, and even presidents of the company, but to no avail. Things were not going to change, and because of my attempts to make changes, the management started to phase me out. I didn't understand why this was happening because I truly loved what I was doing—and to be quite honest, I was good at it.

So, a few years before the pandemic, I walked away from my short seven-year career. Shortly after, I was introduced to Juice Plus, a health and nutrition direct sales company that I am currently working with as a distributor.

Even though I didn't know it at the time, this is how God was in control. God knew how to get me out of this industry that I loved for a purpose. When the pandemic hit Michigan, nursing homes were locked down. Employees were mandated to do things that I would never agree to, sick people were placed into nursing homes with no regard for the safety of staff or other residents, and many people died because of it. God, in His greatness, allowed me to walk away from all that before it happened. He is always in control. We just need to do our part and follow His lead. He has His best plans for us as promised in Jeremiah 29:11.

"For I know the plans I have for you," declares the Lord, "plans to prosper you and not to harm you, plans to give you hope and a future."

God will take us from glory to glory if we are paying attention. For me, glory to glory has to do with my spirituality.

I was born into a Catholic family. We were "average" practicing Catholics. We would all make our sacraments and go to church most of the time. But, of course, we had to go every Christmas and Easter. That was a no-brainer. And yes, we had to get ashes on Ash Wednesday and practice Lent by giving something up, but we were never regular attenders or served the church in any capacity. I was happy growing up Catholic, so that's what we did when we had children.

For me, Catholicism was good, but there were certain things I did not believe. For example, I did not believe that the Pope is infallible, that confession to a Priest "washes" us of our sins, and that during communion, the bread and wine turned into the body and blood of Jesus. Nonetheless, I happily participated and raised my children in the church because I believed it was important for them to have a spiritual foundation.

We went to church as kids because our parents made us go, and we didn't ask questions. I always liked church. In fact, when I was a junior in high school, I contemplated being a nun. I was depressed at the time, riddled with severe acne, and made prayer a priority. I wasn't popular in school and was never pursued by any boys, so being a nun—why not! Ultimately, during my senior year, I decided that being a nun was not my calling—probably when I signed up for the senior class trip.

So here we were, raising our three kids and taking them to church on Sunday, and they never wanted to go. They kept saying, "It's boring." After about a year of struggle, we decided there had to be a better way. There had to be a church that the kids would enjoy. That's when we left the Catholic Church and went to a nondenominational church.

The first service was more like a talk show to me. I was used to hymns, standing up, sitting down, reciting prayers, and a priest leading. Now, this was different. We sang worship songs, and then there was a message, and nothing seemed scripted. We were not comfortable with that first service, but we would give it a second try. Much to our surprise, that would become our church. My kids were actually excited to go, and they decided to follow Jesus there. Our time there would be short-lived as we were about to move again.

We had built our dream house on the west side of Michigan in West Olive. Now, this house was the best! We lived on a swimmable pond stocked with fish and were two miles from miles of Lake Michigan beaches. The location was amazing. We thought my husband would retire there, and that's where we would live. But again, when the plant closed, Steve lost his job.

God always has a plan. His boss had found a new position in Holly, Michigan, and invited him to work there. It was a blessing and a curse. Holly is about 2.5 hours away from our dream home. In our infinite wisdom, we hatched a plan. We had friends that had relocated to Holly. Steve would live with them Monday through Friday and come home on weekends. It was a struggle, but we made it work for about twelve months.

It was then that we decided we had to move, and guess what? That's right when the housing market crashed in 2009. We had an amazing brand-new house. We thought you can't lose money on a new build, but we were wrong. We lost almost $80,000. I knew it was not worth keeping a beautiful house when my family was separated. So, I had to make a long-term decision, knowing that everything was working together for my good.

I still remember standing in the kitchen hugging my then ten-year-old son and crying because we had to leave our dream home. But I remembered hearing the words of a wise woman whom I had befriended: "Laura, it's just a house. Your family needs to be together." So, for the 14th time, we were moving to another city.

We would later regain some of our losses on the flip side when we bought a new home on a short sale, so it all worked out. The house we would eventually find needed some cleaning up, but all in all, it was the perfect house—with everything we needed. There was a master bedroom and a guest bedroom with a bath on the first floor, a finished bonus room, and many more things we were looking for.

Back to the church! This move was no different than the previous ones other than I had one friend in the city. New location, no group of friends, directionally challenged (usually by the time I figured out the city, we were moving again), no job for me, and no church.

We started looking for a church to call home. If you've ever done this, you know it can be difficult. Nothing felt right for a while, but we finally found a church we liked. We attended for a few weeks, and then one Sunday, the congregation was taking a vote on whether to allow the pastor to be a missionary while still leading the church or to release him from his position. They released him, and we no longer had a church to call home. This led us to follow this pastor and be part of a church plant, which is when a group of people comes together under another church to start a new church. We were part of the church called "The Potter's Wheel" in Fenton, MI.

We stayed there for two years and, in the end, had to walk away because our visons did not line up. We were back to searching for a church to call home. We found Cornerstone Church shortly after, and that would be *our* church. It was a big step for us because this church was charismatic. I mean raising your hands, clapping, and services longer than an hour. Wow! Who knew church could be like that?

It was at Cornerstone Church that we would go from glory to glory and deepen our relationship with Jesus. We would receive the gift of speaking in tongues, learn to pray out loud, serve in different ministries, and go on our first mission trip as a family, followed by three more missions.

Through the missions, we were privileged to go to Honduras, Dominican Republic, Peru, and Nicaragua. There we would preach the word of God, meet amazing people, lay hands on the sick and see healings, be a part of the medical team, and serve others with their health needs. We were filled with the Holy Spirit on one mission trip to the Dominican Republic. Yes, these are things that I did not know about, but they became a part of who I am.

We were very happy at this church, and our faith grew by leaps and bounds. But then the pandemic happened. Churches began shutting down and that didn't sit right with us. We wanted to be in church, gathering with friends, worshipping, and praying. We found a church that stayed open, and we thought this was the one—for a short time, until Cornerstone Church would re-open their doors. But as we continued to go, we found that God was again moving us and taking us from glory to glory. Not to say that this was an easy decision as we struggled whether it was us or God moving us. We received assurance that it was God, so we jumped.

Just when I thought I had seen everything, we found a church that would worship like none I'd ever been to before. There would be no time limit on worship. People would jump and clap and dance, and God had grown me to love to worship him in this way. YES, a quiet catholic girl raising her hands, jumping, dancing, and singing—only God can do these things. The name of the Church is Floodgate, in Brighton, Michigan. It was one of only two Michigan churches that stayed open during the pandemic—never shutting their doors and growing from 150 to 1,500 members in a matter of months. Pastor Bill Bolin teamed up with some of his contacts at the State Capital to challenge the executive order issued by the Governor and the order was amended. The church grew so fast, enough services couldn't be added, and they had to buy a new building. Which is in the process of being renovated with a grand opening target of late 2022. It is a church that is alive, holy spirit filled, and on fire for the Lord.

My new experience at Floodgate Church gave me a lot of perspectives. As I looked at how my relationship with God evolved since first being raised as a Catholic, I came to understand that a person's spiritual journey can always grow and evolve. My parents did the best they could with what they knew, and I am forever grateful. In doing so, I've had the privilege to know God my entire life. This has given me the courage to explore different ways to expand my spiritual journey.

I'm not suggesting that you leave your church. However, I do suggest questioning everything, reading the Bible for yourself, and asking God where He wants you to be. There are many ways to worship and express your love for God and so much to learn. Whether you love your current church or not, do not limit yourself or your growth. It sounds cliché, but as you have probably already heard, doing the same thing repeatedly and expecting different results is the definition of insanity. This is true in our spiritual journey as well. Do not limit yourself by recycling your beliefs. Challenge yourself to grow in the spirit.

Even though we are inclined to carry forward the same beliefs as our family, it's not always the wisest choice. Consider this example:

It's Christmas time and Mom is preparing the meal. She takes out a ham and cuts off both ends an places it in the pan. So, Dad asks," Why are you cutting off both ends?" Mom says, "Because that's what my mom does." Then Dad says, " Let's call your mom and ask her why she cuts off both ends." They call the mom, and she says it's because her mom did it. So, then we call Great-Grandma and ask her. She says, "O, that's easy, because the pan was too small."

Sometimes we do things without ever knowing why.

Learn to ask why.

7th Lesson

CHANGE IS GOOD

• • •

"Change is hard at first, messy in the middle,
and gorgeous at the end."
— Robin Sharma

What is one thing we all need to do to grow but most of us don't like to do or go through?

The answer is *change*.

We like to get to a certain point in life where we are comfortable and then stay there uninterrupted, in our bubble of comfort. And why wouldn't we? It feels good, safe, calm, and familiar. But when we get comfortable, we stop growing.

I know that on my journey through life, the many changes I have had to make have kept me out of my comfort zone. They challenged me mentally, emotionally, and spiritually and, in the end, have made me stronger.

As I shared earlier, in my 36 years of marriage with Steve, we have moved a whopping 16 times, and we're not done. Every time we packed up and moved, it was another leap of faith out of my comfort zone. With each new place I got to call home, I had to learn about an entirely new city and community and a whole new state a few times. It seemed like each time when I finally figured out how to live and navigate in a new area, we would once again be moving.

My first move to the tiny trailer (our first place together) in Hinesville, Georgia, was a difficult move for me. I left the comfort of my family and friends and even my job to move to another state. My husband was in the Army, and we couldn't afford the trailer park, so we lived in a ladies' backyard next to the park. There were three old one-bedroom trailers lined up in the backyard. Yes, that was my first place! Steve was so proud of his find. It was only $205 a month—what a deal!

I'm not sure why but I was not part of the decision, and when I arrived, I was less than happy. Thinking about that as I write this book, why wasn't I part of the decision? I do not know to this day. Maybe it was because I was working two jobs and planning the wedding, but I had no part in our housing. Nonetheless, I made the best of it. I decorated with what I had, and our little trailer in the backyard became our first home.

Many changes would be on the horizon for me, but I just didn't know it. After having my first child, my body changed. It went from bad to worse. I was never interested in exercise and health as a young adult; that passion would come later in my life. When I became pregnant, it took four years to figure out how to reduce my post-pregnancy body fat. I don't like to say "lose weight" because often we find the things we lose.

I started going to a gym and working out to reclaim my body. I would do different kinds of cardio and weights, and after about a year, no difference. I didn't know what I was doing, and without someone to show me the proper form and reps, I was not getting any results. I know most of us think we can do it on our own. So, we get a book and skim through the pages to get an idea of what we can accomplish, and then we do it. But I've learned that if you want something that you don't have, it is best to find someone that has already achieved what you want to accomplish and learn from them.

But, of course, this isn't just for health and fitness. The shortcut to any new result in any area of life is to learn from people who have what you want.

Truth be told, most of us don't want to spend the money on a trainer, and that was certainly true for me. It took a year for me to get that credit card out and pay for a personal trainer. It was $75 per training session, two times per week for four months. This girl kicked my butt weekly, and she made sure my form was correct, which is very important. I learned many new ways to transform my body, and as I got stronger and started seeing results, I started working out harder. I started to love going to the gym to get the workouts in. I felt more confident and better than I had in years.

Then, in 2020, I decided to rid my life of all the habits that were interfering with my success. I did this by hiring a mentor to lead me through a personal development program that would transform our lives. To this day, we continue to improve our habits, thoughts, and beliefs so that we can grow and improve and experience more of what life has to offer.

Working with a personal trainer and then a mentor were pivotal steps in my life. It wasn't just the decision to do so that was transformational. There is magic in commitment, especially when that commitment involves money. When finances are tight, spending money on personal growth can be scary, but if you have the faith to believe in the person you will become, then the commitment is worth the risk. From a spiritual point of view, you are demonstrating your faith in God when you commit to personal growth. God is always with us, but it takes courage to believe that He will be there in the future as we work on developing the new and upgraded version of ourselves.

Unfortunately, all too often, we let the lack of money stop us from doing things that could improve our lives or just things we want to do to enjoy life. It is either the lack of money that we let stop us or the fear of scarcity—holding onto what we have because we don't know if we can ever replace that money. Here's an example.

When our children were young, we bought a timeshare that would allow us to go on vacation every year. We would mostly go on spring break when the kids were off school. We were blessed to be able to do this for several years. We would also go to Mexico, the Bahamas, the Dominican Republic, and even Europe. We did not have the money to do these things, but we simply decided to go. Yes, we were in BIG debt, but it never worried me. I knew that we would always be okay.

Now, I am not suggesting that you rack up your credit card and go on vacations. I'm simply telling my story and how it worked out. I am happy and grateful that we lived this way and were able to show our children many different parts of the world. The many memories we made and the different cultures we experienced are priceless.

Change is good. It's not always easy or convenient, but it's good. Why would you want to be the same person tomorrow as you are today? Life has so much to offer. God has given us so many incredible gifts, many of which cannot be received unless we are willing to learn and grow. Yes, just as a child will grow into their new clothing, we have to grow into the many gifts that await us.

When I look at my life with a wide-angle lens, I can see how I have made a lot of small adjustments to make things work. Nonetheless, my big, transformational changes came from moving frequently, exercising, mindset shifts, and even spiritual and religious changes.

Through each of these, I have learned that we should develop the habit of thinking for ourselves and not taking advice from people just because we know them, are related to them, or like them. Instead, by thinking for ourselves, I mean asking the right questions and developing the discernment to only accept advice from people who already have the success we want. We have to remain willing to keep an open mind, learn and try new things, and most importantly, always ask questions that lead to the answers we seek. When asking questions, be resourceful. Use winning words that look for answers rather than justify failure.

WINNING WORDS THAT OPEN YOUR MIND TO POSSIBILITIES

Why can I?

Who can help me?

What do I need to learn?

WORDS THAT JUSTIFY FAILURE

What's wrong with me?

Why do I always fail?

How come no one likes me?

It is easy to do what others tell us without ever questioning them. Most of us do that in our family life every day. We do things that we learned from our parents and never ask why, like the ham story. This happens with religion, too. We are raised with a religion, but we don't know the details of what we believe. It's familiar to us. That's why we believe it.

As I shared earlier, I was raised in a Catholic family. My parents and their parents were Catholic. Therefore, I was raised Catholic. I am thankful that I was because it allowed me to know about God and Jesus from a very young age. But as I got older and began to question certain beliefs and traditions, I learned that they were just that—beliefs and traditions. Although there is nothing wrong with that, I wanted more. I was searching for truth based on God's word—the Bible.

I questioned things, and when they didn't make sense to me, I went in a different direction. This did not come without much disappointment from my immediate family. They wanted me to stay where I was, in the Catholic tradition. It would be like continuing to cut the ends off the ham if you had a bigger pan.

I've learned that as we grow and learn more about life and yearn for new and different experiences, sometimes, our family and friends want to hold us back. Not because they are being mean, but because they are not on the same life journey that I am on. They want comfort, continuity, and familiarity. I had to do what made sense to me, even if my immediate family wasn't happy. It has all worked out to this day. They are all still happily Catholic, and we are joyfully non-denominational. In the end, God loves us all.

HOW DID WE J.U.M.P.?

———•————————•———

Every great move forward in your life
begins with a leap of faith, a step into the unknown.
— Brian Tracy

In the introduction to this book, I asked a curious question: *Have you ever wondered why some married couples live happily ever after, and are still in love and still best friends after many years, while others are unhappily married and counting the days until they are no longer together?*

How did we end up being the "happily ever after" wife and husband?

How did we jump from being 19- and 20-years young, with virtually no life experience, to over 36 years together and maintain the integrity of our relationship?

Even though we didn't have a handbook to make this jump through time, looking back, eight commitments kept us together:

- ✓ Trust God
- ✓ Be on the same page
- ✓ Commit to self-development
- ✓ Surround yourself with only quality people
- ✓ Set written goals
- ✓ Think long-term
- ✓ Have a grateful attitude
- ✓ Make health a priority

TRUST GOD

We have trusted God to make a way even when things seemed uncertain, impossible, or unlikely. We have this trust because we believe God is omnipresent. He is with us in our past, present, and future. He has good plans for our life, and He wants us to have an intimate relationship with Him.

BE ON THE SAME PAGE

Many marriages fail because God is not at the center of the relationship. When it comes to making decisions, we are on the same page. We talk things through, pray, put God first, and then act when we are in agreement with each other. We don't see ourselves as just wife and husband. We believe that we are a cord of three: God, Steve, and Laura

To make a big J.U.M.P., you must be on the same page.

COMMIT TO SELF-DEVELOPMENT

We are committed to personal growth. Working on ourselves, developing our heart, mind, and spirit, getting a mentor, and being open-minded are key to our success. Being willing to spend money on self-development is something we are committed to. If you pay for something, you are more likely to do it.

SURROUND YOURSELF WITH ONLY QUALITY PEOPLE

Nothing is more empowering than surrounding yourself with high-quality, like-minded people who inspire and encourage you to be your best. More so, to associate with people who have accomplished what you want to achieve.

Want better health? Spend time with healthy people and let their good habits rub off on you. Join a gym and get a trainer to help you achieve your goals. Too many times we thought we knew it all and we did not get the results we were looking for.

Want to grow spiritually? Find people who hold the same standards, beliefs, and values as you and challenge you to grow in the spirit. This includes people not in your physical proximity but that you can learn from by immersing yourself in their books, videos, etc.

In short, surround yourself with people who have high standards.

"Show me your friends, and I'll show you your future."

This is hard because sometimes you have to leave people behind who aren't going where you are. That's not to say you still can't be friends, but everyone isn't going where you are going. We have learned that many friends are there for a season and that's ok.

SET WRITTEN GOALS

Write your goals down and review them every morning and evening—first when you wake up and just before you go to bed. Written goals reinforce your beliefs and commitments to yourself and God. You reap what you sow. You sow with written goals.

Steve Harvey is a great example of the power of written goals. He was homeless, broke, and lost his family, but he had a dream written on paper, and he had faith in God. Now you see Steve Harvey on TV—many times a day.

Michael Jordan is another great example. He was cut from the varsity team his sophomore year in high school, but that did not stop him. He worked harder and believed until his effort and belief became his reality. Of course, any one of us can be successful and do amazing things. If you can see it in your mind, you can be it.

THINK LONG TERM

Don't get caught up in the petty distractions of life. Stay focused on your outcome and understand that God works in the moment and long-term. Consistency is everything. Believe that everything will work out even when you can't see it now. God knows what you are capable of, but He cannot do the work for you. You have to demonstrate your faith and take the appropriate action.

We are doing this right now. We are staying the course. We are writing this book, working on our self—mind, body, and spirit. The

Bible says in Romans 12:2: "Do not be conformed to this world; be transformed by the renewing of your mind, that you may prove what is the good and acceptable and perfect will of God."

Renewing our mind daily is one the disciplines we strive to achieve.

HAVE A GRATEFUL ATTITUDE

Have an attitude of gratitude. Be grateful every day for everything you have. It's so easy to forget to be grateful. How many times do you leave for work and open the garage door? Come home from work and open the garage door? When that door breaks, what do we do? Complain, get mad, get upset? The one time it breaks, we forget about the thousands of times it worked.

Gratitude is not just being thankful for what you have but also for what is coming. When you can feel genuine gratitude for what is coming into your life, but you don't yet have, you communicate your faith and belief to God.

MAKE HEALTH A PRIORITY

Your experience of life is only as good as the quality of your health. Your ability to see, taste, touch, smell, hear, think, and feel, is nothing short of the greatest of miracles. Instead of waiting for God to perform a miracle in your life, realize that your body is the miracle, and He will bless you by you putting to use the miracle of your body.

Take care of your health. If you do not take care of your body, where else can you live? Health is more important than financial riches. What good is it if you have all the money in the world but feel like crap?

At the same time, money does buy health. Money will allow you to buy better quality food, get better health care, and even allow for preventative care. If you develop the habit of making health a priority, you will have the energy to create the life you desire. Exercising daily, eating right, drinking water, reducing stress, and getting quality sleep are all important. Every day, make time for your health.

• • • • •

We have gone a long distance with those eight commitments and have developed a lot of spiritual traction over our 36 years. God and life have been good to us.

EPILOGUE

Writing this book and sharing my story has been an incredible exercise in gratitude. When Steve and I first met, we were so young and had our entire lives ahead of us. From high school kids to joining the military and starting a family, and everything between, it has been a bountiful 36 years. There were a lot of ups and downs, mishaps, and mistakes, but the amount of love and faith between our hearts made up for any misfortunes.

Looking back now, it's incredible how much our lives have transformed since we first met—especially our spiritual beliefs and faith. We have had so much to be grateful for, and we continue to be blessed in this new stage of our lives.

We had no idea what life, and God, had in store for us. There was no way to know. We just knew we had to put one foot in front of the other and keep moving forward.

But writing this book put everything in perspective. All of my life makes sense. Everything I have been through, and everything we have been through as husband and wife, has come together in God's divine plan. I can see how all the pieces fit together and how God used everything for His glory.

Jesus is the central figure in my life—our lives. After all our years of struggles and blessings, we now see how he is using all of what we have been through to unleash our potential and give us a greater sense of purpose.

The seven insights are only a fraction of what I have learned over these 36+ years, but they are of incredible importance and significance:

1. Leap And Grow Your Wings
2. Mindset Matters
3. God Loves Goals
4. "Believe"

5. Words Have Power
6. God Is In Control
7. Change Is Good

There is so much more that could have been written, but I have done my best to share the most meaningful stories to honor my husband and the gift of love and family that he has given me, and to honor our Lord and Savior, Jesus.

BOOK TWO

•————————————•

Navigating the Miracles

STEVE ALLMEN

Steve's Introduction 71

Mindset is Everything 77

Happiness is a Choice 83

Words Are Powerful 93

Power of Words Exercise 105

Faith Over Fear 107

Reflect and Move Forward 109

Knowing–Doing Gap 119

Your Perception is Your Truth 123

Epilogue 129

INTRODUCTION

Have you ever felt like you are on an amusement park ride and can't get off?

Does your day look something like this:

Wake up, go to work for longer than you want, come home, eat a late dinner, say hello to the children for an hour, go to bed—repeat.

I call this the hamster wheel of life, where we trade our time and life for money. It doesn't have to look like this. There is a way to create the life you want and live it the way you want, with the results you desire.

I'm one of those people, perhaps just like you, who got tired of being tired, and I finally got off the wheel. My transition wasn't graceful or smooth, but it was intentional. Making changes in life—BIG changes—is not always easy or convenient, but when the need for change is staring you in the face, it's worth the discomfort. My story is what that transition looked like living my life as a Christian. My spiritual beliefs didn't make things easier. They just made them possible, and the results have been greater than I ever imagined.

Just like most people, I was raised to believe if you go to school, get a degree, and work hard, the rewards you seek in life will be there for you. I had seen this pattern with my family, my father, uncles, and aunts, all doing it with different degrees of success.

Most of my life I lacked confidence and had an underlying belief that I was not good enough. As a child, I wasn't popular, strong, fast, or the smartest in the class. I was an introvert. I only had one or two friends that I would speak with, and rarely would I ask a question in a group setting.

When I met my wife Laura things started to open for me. She pushed me to be more outgoing and more engaging. Her tenacity was an example for me and stretched my mind and my belief in myself.

When I say tenacity, I mean she never accepted any excuses from me.

In my first year of college, I was busy making money, hanging out with a group of friends that were going nowhere, and chasing Laura, who would later become my wife, while losing focus on my studies.

The first semester, I passed one class and failed four others. During the second semester, I continued the same path but received a call from a recruiter. I said yes, I would come in to listen—something I swore I would never do in high school. The day I went, I remember telling Laura, "Don't worry, I'm not joining, just listening." Several hours later, I returned, enlisted in the United States Army.

Remember the tenacity I spoke of in Laura? That same tenacity would bubble up during my basic training. I would receive several letters from her each day. Being a guy in basic training who was not the best physical specimen, I was busy. I didn't return the favor to her by writing back. But, somehow, she was able to get through many channels and talk directly to my drill sergeant. From that point on through the remainder of boot camp, I had to deliver letters to him with my feet on his desk, doing elevated pushups.

At another point in time, I was sent to Korea. We had been married only a few short months. When soldiers go to Korea, they are not authorized to bring their families. Within a few months, Laura had worked the channels, pleading with representatives and congressmen to allow her to come join me. I was on a 12-month tour. Laura spent seven of those months with me in Korea.

Looking back on those early years, I can connect the dots and understand how God was working in our lives. God brought Laura to me on my senior trip in high school, and we have grown together ever since. It was a divine appointment for sure.

As Christians, God is the central figure in our life and all our decisions. Since God is an integral part of my story and mentioned throughout the book, here is what I believe:

God is alive, the creator of the universe, and we are created in His image. He has a plan and purpose for each of us. God loves us and wants each of us to have an intimate relationship with Him. I believe in the trinity: the Father, the Son (Jesus), and the Holy Spirit. Each is equally God, possessing one divine nature. Each is a different role to one another. God the Father is the supreme authority. Jesus is the Son under the Father's authority seeking to do His will. The Holy Spirit resides within us and empowers us to proclaim the Gospel. For clarity, throughout the book, I will use God, Lord, and Jesus interchangeably.

Through our 35+ years of marriage, we have moved 16 times. Each move had a purpose. Each move allowed me to grow individually and spiritually. Each move brought me to a place that allowed me to work on my self-confidence, my ability to speak in front of others, and my ability to be a leader—and brought both of us closer to Jesus.

Our first move was to a 14 by 50 one-bedroom trailer next to a trailer park. I had so little money that I couldn't even afford a place in the trailer park. This is where we spent our first months being married. We had no plan or vision when we said yes, and we didn't even know each other's dreams. We were in love and knew that marriage was the logical next step.

The months we spent in the trailer were filled with ups and downs. I was not a nice person for sure. At one point, Laura packed her car and was leaving to return home to Michigan from Georgia. The problem was, she didn't know how to get out of the town. I found her at a Walmart parking lot and took her car keys. But through faith, forgiveness, and humbleness, we made it through.

When in Korea, I re-enlisted with a guarantee to return to Georgia, where I returned to college to pursue a business degree. One of the projects was to do a business plan, so I completed a project to open a restaurant.

Orders were issued that required me to travel to Germany for four years. To fulfill these, it meant I would have to re-enlist again. It was decision time. Do we go and make the military a career or choose to end our enlistment and request an early exit?

Having had our first baby during this time, we thought it would be best to get out. So, I began to use the business plan project as a tool to open a restaurant and stay in Georgia. Things were lining up to make this happen. However, something in my gut said don't do it. I listened to my gut (the Holy Spirit, I would later learn) and left for Michigan. Three months later, the first Gulf War broke out. My restaurant would have never opened. Over half of the local businesses went out of business as the entire base was deployed.

Several of our future moves contained lessons and opportunities similar to what we learned between Georgia and Michigan. Looking back now, it's easy to see how each had their intertwined lessons. Each relocation came with many decisions, all of which brought growth and confidence.

Looking in the rear-view mirror of my life, if I were to consolidate my many experiences into core life lessons, these are seven that have had the greatest impact:

1. Mindset is everything
2. Happiness is a choice
3. Words are powerful
4. Faith over fear
5. Reflect and move forward
6. Knowing-doing gap
7. Your perception is your truth

When I mentioned getting off the hamster wheel wasn't graceful or smooth, it's because I have learned that life's struggles are the seeds for personal growth, and God uses our difficulties to help us grow in the spirit. There is no other way to authentically share how I got off the hamster wheel and discovered these powerful lessons than through the backdrop of my story.

1st Lesson

MINDSET IS EVERYTHING

• • •

"It is not in the stars to hold
our destiny but in ourselves."
— William Shakespeare

Have you ever noticed that some people bounce back quickly and easily from setbacks and failures and even grow stronger? Yet others never recover or become seemingly sheepish?

Why is there such a big difference in responses to adversity?

The answer is simple.

Mindset.

Yes, "mindset" is a very common buzzword these days, and I used to feel as if it were a bit overused. But, as I look back to understand what brought me to where I am today, the term is extremely important and relevant, especially when living or pursuing a successful life.

Through my experiences, I have come to recognize mindset as your system of thinking and solving problems and how you respond to the circumstances of life. It is your overall attitude toward life. Your mindset drives how you perceive and respond to the situations you encounter.

Here's the definition of mindset from Dictionary.com: "A fixed mental attitude or disposition that predetermines a person's responses to and interpretations of situations."

Your mindset is closely associated with your paradigms. This is something that Bob Proctor has spoken about in-depth. Your paradigms are mini programs running in your subconscious mind that put your life on autopilot. They are like mini mental habits that govern your choices and behavior.

> *"Paradigms are a multitude of habits that guide*
> *every move you make. They affect the way you eat,*
> *walk, and even the way you talk. They govern your*
> *communication, work habits, successes, and failures.*
> *For the most part, your paradigms didn't originate*
> *with you. They're the accumulated inheritance of other*
> *people's habits, opinions, and belief systems. Yet they*
> *remain the guiding force in YOUR life."*
> — *Bob Proctor*

Your mindset and your paradigm determine how you see things. Whether you are looking at a problem or a solution, the attitude you use to approach the situation will define the answer.

For example, if your attitude is that things are okay, they will stay okay. If your attitude is that things are bad, things will continue to be bad. If your attitude is that things are good, they will continue to be good. By changing your attitude, your results can change.

Paradigm = Mindset = Attitude = Outcome

You can have either a positive or negative mindset. A positive mindset believes that everything will work out in the long run. A negative mindset is more pessimistic, hesitant, and does not expect things to work out. If your mindset is generally negative, you will experience more negative emotions and miss out on opportunities because your negativity will blind you to what is possible. If you have a positive mindset, you will believe in possibilities. You will be open to trying new things, willing to learn from your mistakes, and grow through challenges.

There are a variety of different mindsets. Here's a few that you may be familiar with.

Growth mindset: *People who are committed to personal growth*

Fear mindset: *Too much focus on what could go wrong rather than how to succeed.*

Gratitude mindset: *Intentionally focusing on what you are grateful* *for, rather than what is missing from your life.*

Here is an example of how my mindset affected my career.

In 2008 I was in a tumultuous situation in my job. I had just finished closing a manufacturing facility that I had been blessed to be a part of for several years. The team I was on had taken on a faltering, non-profiting factory and turned it around. Under our watch it became an example for lean manufacturing and was respected for earning profit.

We had developed a relationship with a new customer and would take on lower volume projects if there were technological opportunities. Programs that were deemed unprofitable by our sister divisions became diamonds under our watch. We expanded quickly, filled capacity, and delivered on our customer commitments.

The problem: we became victims of the automotive industry crash of 2008-2010. Beginning in 2007, things began to turn south in a hurry. There were three divisions, all operating within an hour-and-a-half of one another, making virtually the same type of products for similar customers.

Ultimately, the success of the division I was part of did not matter. There was excess capacity, and our site was the least costly to close and combine with other divisions. Our division was shut down at the end of 2007.

What I did in the situation was to take on the mindset of a victim. Refusing to see the big picture and unwilling to take a step backward in my position, I joined most of the top management with an assignment to close the division. If successful, I would receive a lump sum bonus if I stayed until the end. I was looking at the glass half empty.

I had assumed there was no room at the top management level within the division. It was hard to understand why, with the results we had delivered, they wanted to shut things down. Throughout the closing process, our team worked well together—diligently doing the right thing to support our people by helping them manage transfer decisions, and work with customers and other divisions to transfer the business.

Of course, we would have daily pity parties behind closed doors about how unfair it was and how the management above us clearly didn't understand the effects of what was being done. Our mindset was certainly cementing our future—where the rainbow would be ending for us.

As I reflect on what happened, several good things came from the closure. Most every hourly person was offered a transfer to work with one of the other divisions, and the lower-level supervision, technical, and support staff had the same opportunity.

Throughout the plant closure, I was identified as a potential candidate to move with some of the business. During my interview with the new management team, my mindset was counter-productive and created feedback that I wasn't qualified. It was crazy. The feedback that I was not qualified was shocking to me, my direct manager, and the next management level. Add to that, the position ahead of me was a step backward from what I was doing, and I am confident I could have helped move the team forward with a huge measure of success, except that I had no vision, no charisma, no life.

Looking back on the situation months later, I knew that I had entered that interview with a mindset that they owed this to me. I would not give them any information, as I wanted them to have to learn the product, the process, and the customer—all the hard way. So, I left the interview without providing them with any expectation of results, leadership, creativity, or vision casting that I could deliver for them.

Mindset is everything! The company thought enough of me that they were willing to provide an opportunity for me to stay with them to help. I am sure the management did not want to consolidate, yet market conditions mandated it. They were making the best decision they thought possible to maintain a competitive position in the marketplace. I could have looked at it with gratitude as an opportunity to prove my commitment to the company, bringing my skillsets to the other division and working to improve myself and the team. I could have accepted the coal and worked to turn it into a diamond, yet I didn't.

Ultimately, my mindset drove me on a different path. Fortunately, the company thought enough of me to offer a role as a program manager, a temporary assignment launching new technology for the group. After receiving this assignment, I was still spiteful toward the company. Unfortunately, I didn't see the situation as an opportunity to prove myself. This assignment led to me traveling internationally for large amounts of time over the next six months, taking more precious time away from my family.

I created a level of resentment and searched for other positions in the area willing to pay the salary I was making. Taking on this negative, entitled mindset took a toll on me. Instead of going all-in towards what I was doing, as I had always done with any position, I found myself inventing things to do when not traveling overseas. I would leave early and invent trips to take so that I could go home, work on projects, and see my children because clearly, they owed me the time from my travel. So, the person I was cheating was myself because I lacked purpose, a sense of achievement and fulfillment—and again, no vision.

Had I approached the situation with a different mindset, I would have been able to learn new technology, work with new suppliers, and establish new relationships. I could have developed my team-building skills, provided value, and served the company. Many people would have been grateful for the opportunity I had been handed, especially during that time in our industry. However, I didn't see it that way.

Completely unaware someone had seen something in me and created this opportunity to keep me on board, I squandered it. The assignment was coming to a close by the end of 2008. I had been offered a position to stay on with the company taking two steps back in status and about a 25% cut in pay, which I gracefully declined. The opportunity was there, but my mindset prevented me from seeing any intrinsic value.

I have since learned my lesson and do things differently. Now, when situational conflict arises, I take the approach of searching for a solution instead of blaming and running. I have learned that our minds can only focus on one thing. Most will focus on the problem, as I had done in the past. We all have problems, and what each of us chooses to do with the problems defines our future. By focusing on solutions, I have found that with the right mindset, good will come regardless of the situation.

Looking back on the plant closure, I realize it was a problem. However, one of the factors that drove my glass-half-empty mindset was that I had a paradigm of limited thinking. I didn't have a larger goal. Without something to focus on, my mind reverted to being concerned with things that would never happen, things in the past, or things that I could not control. It's cliché but true: an idle mind is the devil's workshop.

Today, I have written goals. I take time each day to work on ideas that will help me achieve my goals. I have found that spending time doing this drives my thinking and actions towards the goal. When a problem arises that stops my progress, I search for the solution.

Look at it in this light. If you are driving to a destination and road construction has closed the road you are traveling, you have two choices. You could turn around and go back to where you started or find an alternate route to get you to your destination? You also have a choice about your attitude toward this situation. You could become frustrated (negative mindset) because your plans were interrupted, or you could simply adapt (positive mindset) and change your approach.

Mindset matters.

HAPPINESS IS A CHOICE

• • •

Happiness is a choice, not a result.
Nothing will make you happy
until you choose to be happy.
— Ralph Marston

Ultimately, your mindset is a choice, and all choices have either beneficial or detrimental consequences. They either lead to happiness or dissatisfaction.

This idea of consequences is similar to the biblical concept that you reap what you sow. It's also akin to the idea of karma and the law of cause and effect. In simple terms, for every action, there is a corresponding reaction.

For years, I was oblivious to the knowledge that there were books written about these mindset concepts. There are motivational speakers, lecture series, and centuries of collective wisdom and quotes that talk about the power of the mind, attitude, and beliefs. I suppose I knew that my choices had consequences, but I never really took the time to understand the effect of my choices.

Bob Proctor, one of my favorite mindset teachers, goes into great depth about the law of cause and effect. He cites it as being one of seven natural laws—laws created by God—that are the basis of how our day-to-day life unfolds. Here are two great quotes from the Proctor-Gallagher website.

"Everything in the entire universe happens according
to Law—there is no such thing as chance. Every effect
(result) must have a cause, and that cause must have

an effect. Thus, we have the perpetual, never-ending
cycle of cause and effect."
"Ralph Waldo Emerson called the Law of Cause
and Effect "the Law of Laws." This Law decrees that
whatever you send into the Universe comes back."

If you are not familiar with Bob Proctor, I highly recommend looking for his videos online. Even though I did not discover his teachings until 2020—well after Laura and I first met—understanding the Law of cause and effect has helped me make sense of my life and the effects of many of my choices. In fact, let's wind the clock back a bit to our early days as an example of how the law of cause and effect showed up in our lives and how I discovered that happiness is a choice.

• • • • •

Laura and I meet in high school on our senior class trip at the Voyager Hotel in Daytona Beach, Florida. I had a girlfriend at the time. I remember, clear as the print in this book, the moment Laura walked in through the hotel door. I was instantly taken in by her smile, how she looked, and her uplifting energy. I was sitting at a table with some of my friends and some of her friends, desperately hoping, like most teenage boys on a senior trip, that one of them would fancy me. But when she entered, that all stopped. Those feelings that butterfly feeling is what I thought happiness was. Not to diminish that magical moment, but I have found that it is not.

It's amazing what some people will do to get what they want. In the summer of 1984, I was chasing hard after my wife-to-be. I thought she was rich. After all, the way she was dressed, how she handled herself, the friends she had, she must be. When we returned from Florida, I broke up with my girlfriend, who was Italian and lived in a fancy part of town. I dropped her like a lead balloon. God had a plan. I just was not aware of it, nor even close to being tuned into it.

As things progressed, I discovered that Laura's family did not come from money. Nope, just like me, she was from a middle-class family; both parents worked to make ends meet and do their best to provide for their family. That didn't stop me.

In the weeks immediately following the senior trip, Laura was looking for a prom date; someone to use as bait to make the person whom she liked jealous. Yes, I was the bait—blind and not thinking, just chasing that butterfly happiness. Well, she did get her prom date. I so wanted to please her; I even wore the white tuxedo complete with powder blue bow tie and cummerbund that she wanted, even though it went against every grain of style that I had.

Looking back, I am sure the light yellow four-door Plymouth Volare I borrowed from my parents was not quite the ride she had dreamed of escorting her to the prom. Reflecting on those times, it's amazing how much my style was transforming because of Laura's influence on me. The more time I would spend with her, the more she shopped with me, the more I would transform. Funny, it seemed as though we were buying clothes all the time for me to wear, not her—not sure why.

I remember one night we went on a date: dinner and a movie. I showed up in jeans and one of those three-quarter sleeve length T-shirts that were popular in the '80s. It was probably my pink sleeve concert shirt from Def Leopard. When I was at the door, she looked at me and said, *"We are not going out together with you looking like that. Go home and change into the turquoise parachute pants and black shirt we bought. Then we can go out."*

Here, I had a choice—one that, if you are married and a man, you can likely relate to. I could choose to be stubborn and show her who's in charge by refusing to change, or, for the sake of salvaging the evening and ensuring we would have a fun night, take 15 minutes to drive home, change, and drive back. It would only set us back about 45 minutes.

So, I chose to drive home and change. I didn't realize it at the time, but small decisions like this were preparing me for some of the hills and valleys we would experience in the future.

When I look back to those early days of courting, I now understand that many times I had made choices in the moment that either helped to drive feelings of happiness or created tension. For example, there were plenty of times, perhaps too many, where I felt that my opinion of what was right or how something was to be done was more important than Laura's opinion (I don't recommend that sort of thinking to anyone that is dating or married.) I asked myself the following question:

Am I choosing to have a happy marriage, or am I trying to feed my pride and need for significance?

Being together now for 36 years, I have learned that my need to be right was not always a good choice or strategy when it came to the happiness in our relationship. I now understand that being of value and serving her provides us both happiness. I also understand that the outcome of each day is a product of the choices I make, the words I use, the emotions I display, and the actions I take.

Stepping back to our early years of marriage, Laura and I were learning each other's trigger points; what we liked and what we didn't like. I was 19, and she was 20. Being so young, we took a very common approach based on our mental and emotional maturity. I don't know whether you can relate, but in most cases, if not all, I was right in my mind, and she was right in her mind. And when our needs to be right were not in alignment with one another, it was emotional volcano season.

In our first year of marriage, I was a terrible husband. In writing this book, it opened my mind to understand just how extremely selfish I was.

Before we get into this next section, I thought it appropriate to say:

Laura, If I haven't apologized for what I put you through in those first few years, I apologize now. Yes, I am here on my knees saying sorry, singing "Always and Forever" to you. I am grateful that you chose to hang on. Somehow, you knew there was a bigger plan.

I love and appreciate Laura for putting up with all the turmoil that I caused. When we lived in the one-bedroom 14 by 50 trailer in a lady's backyard, next to the trailer park which was too pricey for me, that was a big sacrifice for her because it was not an ideal place to live. She moved from Michigan to Georgia and had no friends. I worked shifts, 4 a.m. to 1 p.m., or 10 a.m. to 7 p.m. On the 10 a.m. days, I had to report for Physical Training on the Army base at 6 a.m. So, most of her time was spent alone in that less than adequate home. That was true love and dedication.

Unfortunately, I made it worse for her. On the days that I only worked until 1 p.m., I would stay after and play racquetball or basketball with the boys, as I had done before we were married. She would get so mad at me, and I simply didn't see anything wrong with what I was doing. We would argue so much. There were times she was so mad at me that she would go weeks without speaking to me—literally. I could only imagine what her mother thought.

What I learned from this is that when we make choices, we are also choosing the consequences that come with that choice. When we were dating, I had to choose to make sacrifices in how I dressed, whom I hung out with, or how I drove, all to make her happy. I did it for her and for me, and in return, I was happy. So much so that we both said yes to marriage.

In those early years, probably because of my young level of maturity, many of my choices came with the consequences of hurting Laura emotionally. This cost us intimacy and opportunities to truly discover who we were and what our dreams were together. There were many times when I had chosen the gratification of doing what I wanted to for my own short-term happiness rather than considering Laura's feelings and what was best for both of us. In those instances, being "happy" came at a great price.

What I have since discovered is that true happiness is a sense of joy, fulfillment, contentment, and feeling good about your life that comes through honoring your partner and God.

Ephesians 5:25-28:{25} Husbands, love your wives, as Christ loved the church and gave himself up for her, {26} that he might sanctify her, having cleansed her by the washing of water with the word, {27} so that he might present the church to himself in splendor, without spot or wrinkle or any such thing, that she might be holy and without blemish. [a] {28} In the same way, husbands should love their wives as their own bodies. He who loves his wife loves himself.

I was far from this. In fact, things just got worse. Before even seeing our one-year anniversary, the Army gave me orders that would send me to Korea, with the potential to be assigned anywhere in the country, including the Demilitarized Zone (DMZ). Adding to the complexity, Laura could not accompany me as I was not an officer.

In reflection, I can see how this assignment was God's hand working in our lives. He knew that we would not stay together much longer with my behavior, and He had great plans for us, so He provided a path that could create an opportunity for me to change direction. Initially, the absence brought us closer. But as time went on, I picked right back up with my selfish behavior.

We would talk on the phone for hours. Almost every call ended in some type of argument. We had phone bills of more than $600 that Laura would work so hard to pay. As she was doing that, I was reckless, chasing the bar scene and running with the boys. She was such a fighter. Somehow, she opened the channels to be able to come to Korea.

Did I mention that I am sorry for how I acted and treated you?

I found an upper flat off the base to rent, received permission from the local command for her to be there, and she made plans to show up at my door. Even her arrival in Korea was an event that proved to be selfish on my part.

The day she was flying in, I had planned for a flight to meet her in Seoul, Korea, based on when she was scheduled to arrive. My assignment had me based in Pusan, Korea, which had flights going to Seoul virtually every hour. Knowing this, on the day she was to arrive, I found some time to play basketball with the boys after work, leaving just enough time to grab a taxi and get to the airport to catch a flight. I was clueless, unaware, and clearly centered on myself.

Thunderstorms were in the forecast and coming quickly. If I had checked the weather earlier that morning, I could have known to leave early to ensure that I would be there to meet her as she got off the plane. After all, she was traveling to another country for the first time ever.

When I arrived at the airport, I quickly found that my flight was delayed due to the weather. Within a couple of hours, all flights had been canceled. My alternative was to take a train. It was a four-to-six-hour train ride, and her plane was scheduled to land while I would have been enroute. This was life before cell phones, so if I was on the train, there would be no way for us to connect. So, I chose not to travel but to leave word with the airlines to have a note for her to call my dorm phone. This turned out to be a very poor decision.

Laura's flight arrived extremely late because of the weather; so late, in fact, that customs was closed. She was not allowed to access the content of her luggage and was taken to a hotel near the airport. She struggled with communication as most, if not all, of the people trying to explain what was happening could not speak English. When we finally spoke, she was in tears, not knowing where she was or why I was not there, as the note I had provided was lost in translation.

Because of this unpleasant situation, this led to the first time I had ever had a conversation with her father where his language was such that I am choosing not to repeat it here. I felt terrible, though I was arguing my point as to why I was right for not being there.

The next morning, she arrived on the first flight to Pusan. Not the vision of welcome she or I had of celebrating her arrival. The next several months were filled with highs and lows, many more lows than highs, as I had not figured out how to treat her.

She returned home from Korea a month or so before I did. When I returned, I believe this was the turning point for me. We were in our second year of marriage. We were on leave awaiting a new assignment that I had re-enlisted for, to return to the base we left in Georgia. During this leave, I decided that I wanted to be married and that I wanted that marriage to be with Laura.

Now, things didn't turn instantly rosy. In fact, it took about seven years to fully understand and strive to become what the Lord tells us in Ephesians. But by making the decision, I found that my thoughts, emotions, and actions were becoming aligned with being a loving husband. The more that I strove to serve and sacrifice myself for us, the more we were able to experience happiness.

In fact, I remember one day I was riding in our minivan with our three children, mad at Laura, discussing with them how I was right, and she had no reason to be mad. One of them, my daughter, I think, said, "Dad, remember what you told us: *'Do you want to be right, or do you want to be happy?'*"

When I heard the words, immediately the lightbulb turned on. Our choices have consequences. It is up to us whether the consequence is positive or negative. With this epiphany, three questions came to mind:
1. How do we want to perceive a situation?
2. How do we want to react to someone's actions?
3. How do we want to show our love to our neighbors?

Here are my thoughts about these questions.

How do we want to perceive a situation?

Thinking about the early days of our marriage, if I had taken the time to look at situations through her eyes, I am sure that my perception and many of my choices would have been much different. She loved me and wanted to serve me. I didn't give her the opportunity. My perception was that what I was doing—my job, my hobbies, and my time—was more important than serving her. My decisions set in motion consequences that put significant strain on our relationship. I later discovered that by taking time to talk, listen with intent, and bringing a desire to serve her, I was able to understand the effects of my choices.

How do we want to react to someone's actions?

When Laura and I were in Korea, we fought like cats and dogs. Ugly really. What I found is that hurt people typically hurt people. The choices I made provided negative consequences. Laura was hurt, and as I was not coming from a place of love, honor, and respect, I was reacting.

Today, I understand that, regardless of the situation, whether someone is screaming at me or not talking to me, how I react will drive consequences into the situation. Instead of trading words for words and fire for fire, I now work to come from a position of humility and love.

Regardless of whether I believe that I am right or wrong, I find a way to be apologetic or empathetic. When the situation is diffused, I reflect to understand if there was something I said or did that had provoked the action. Was there a miscommunication? I work to gain understanding and improve my actions, my words, and my thinking to bring more to our relationship.

How do we want to show our love to our neighbors?

When I first asked myself this question, I treated it in a physical context. In all the 16+ moves Laura and I made, we had a lot of different neighbors. Looking back on each situation, it was rare that we ever established a relationship with the person or people who lived next door, below or above us. I think this was primarily due to the choices I made.

Often my priorities were out of alignment. I found myself consistently making my career my priority. I traded too many hours at the office, plant, or on business trips, in exchange for any real relationships outside of the office. In addition, I was kind of an introvert, never really seeking conversation or opportunity to meet or serve alongside people. Again, I was always focused on myself and my family.

The older I get, the more I find myself getting to know my neighbors. I think the driver for this is my growth in understanding the importance of having relationships with others.

I remember my first men's bible study group, which was a stretch for me to commit to participating in. We read the book *The Measure of a Man: Twenty Attributes of a Godly Man, by Gene A. Getz.*

Two critical points became clear to me in this study.
- First, as men, we need to have a close circle of like-minded friends who are willing to hold us accountable.
- Second, we need to understand that our actions and the results of our choices speak louder than any words we utter.

I also came to realize that my children are a mirror of me and my mindset. They emulate my words and my actions. I remember always telling them to reach out to others to develop relationships, to find friends to confide in, and how important it is to have relationships, yet I had never done the same. My actions and results were not consistent with my words, and they could see it, and so they did not take my advice to heart.

Now that I am growing mentally and emotionally, I have found that the more inclusive I am with others, the more I am there to listen and serve people, the more my love grows—not just for them but for all people.

Through purposefully taking myself out of my comfort zone, by actively engaging in conversations with others, I have begun to develop new relationships. This new emotional courage is making a difference in my children. I can see glimpses of them beginning to do what I am now doing, not what I was saying.

Taking purposeful action has brought both points from the Bible study into my world. The choices I make to seek, listen, and serve my neighbor, shape the consequences from my actions.

Today, my neighbor means anyone the Lord brings across my path, providing an opportunity to add value to their lives. For each person I meet, I engage with the intention of adding value and leaving them better than before we met.

If we love our neighbors, treat them as we would wish to be treated, speak as we would want to be spoken to, and help as we would want to have others help. It is amazing the transition that will occur in your heart when you do these.

Through our choices is where we will determine the consequences. Sometimes, even when we are right, the battle to prove so is not worth the cost of the war.

WORDS ARE POWERFUL

• • •

"Words have energy and power with the ability to help,
to heal, to hinder, to hurt, to harm, to humiliate,
and to humble."
— *Yehuda Berg*

Have you ever had your feelings hurt by something that was said to you?

Has someone ever said something that made you feel happy, confident, proud, or loved?

Where do those feelings come from? Can another person actually hurt your feelings or make you feel good about yourself?

No.

Only in the last few years did I become aware of the true power of our words.

Contrary to what most people understand, our feelings are an effect of what we have agreed to believe. If you allow someone else to hurt your feelings, you have given them authority over your feelings and self-image. You do not have to believe or agree with anything that anyone says, and not everything that is said requires a reaction. The only thing that truly matters is what you think and believe about yourself. Words have power, but they only have the power that you give them.

What you speak and how you respond to what is spoken has a lot to do with your childhood. When we are kids, our minds are little sponges. We soak up everything we hear from our environment, especially from the people closest to us— parents, teachers, relatives, religious leaders. If these people have a positive mindset, it will rub off on us. The same is true if they had a negative mindset. They duplicate their thinking habits and patterns into ours. As we grow, our adult mindset is the product of those early influences.

Can you recall things that were said to you as a kid that affect how you think now?

While growing up, I remember hearing many different sayings (idioms) meant to be inspiring guide stones. In reality, many of them were setbacks. Here's two examples.

"MONEY DOESN'T GROW ON TREES."

Who grew up learning money doesn't grow on trees? Most of us were told this when money was tight. The intention may have been good, to teach us to be financially responsible, but the consequence is that we learned to believe money is scarce, which it is not. Oddly, we weren't taught where money does grow—through many paths including being a business owner or investor.

When we are kids, the analogy can be confusing. Of course, money doesn't grow on trees, but what does? Fruit, nuts, seeds. It would have been the perfect opportunity to teach us an analogy between how things work in nature and real life.

For example, there must first be a seed planted in the ground for a tree to grow. It must be planted at the right depth and have access to water and proper soil to take root and grow.

The fruit doesn't come right away. The tree first must mature, which may take several years. Each fruit begins as a flower. Once pollenated, it takes the right mixture of water, sun, and temperature to grow into a piece of fruit. If it gets too cold or hot, or not enough water, the flower may never blossom into fruit, or it may yield a small harvest.

Each variety of tree may grow at a different rate, provide a different amount of fruit, and produce for a different time. The ability of any individual tree to successfully bear fruit is determined by the environment in which it grows.

The fruit in your life is the money, friendships relationships, experiences, spiritual and overall beliefs—all of which are most certainly influenced by how you were raised, the words that were spoken into your life, and how you were taught to think.

Here are two bible verses that are helpful in making this point.

"It was planted in good soil beside abundant waters, that it might yield branches and bear fruit and become a splendid vine." —Ezekiel 17:8

"A farmer went out to plant his seed. He scattered the seed on the ground. Some fell on a path. Birds came and ate it up. Some seeds fell on rocky places where there wasn't much soil. The plants came up quickly because the soil wasn't deep. When the sun came up, it burned the plants. They dried up because they had no roots. Other seeds fell among thorns. The thorns grew up and crowded out the plants. Still, other seeds fell on good soil. It produced a crop of 100, 60, or 30 times more than what was planted. Those who have ears should listen and understand." —Mathew 13:1-9

You can't plant a seed one day and expect fruit the next day. This is also true about life. It takes time and patience to nurture relationships, grow businesses and investments, and turn ideas into reality.

A farmer can't just think about his crops and hope that they grow, or water the fields when he feels like it. He must be consistent. Similarly, the more you think about and focus on your ideas and keep your emotions in alignment with what you are trying to create, the more likely you are to act. If you put in little effort, you will get little results. Conversely, if you put in a lot of disciplined effort and maintain your tenacity in achieving the goal, you can achieve exponential results.

Words truly have power. Your patterns of thinking, habits, daily rituals, and beliefs are the fruit of the words that have been spoken into your life that you believed and allowed to become a part of your identity. The way you talk to yourself is also shaped by those same influences, as is the way you communicate, and the expectations you place on yourself and others. Even your level of confidence is a by-product of the words spoken into your life that you accepted as truth.

For me, my spiritual beliefs changed and evolved as I listened to and allowed strong Christian spiritual leaders to speak into and influence my thinking, values, and personal standards.

Since I have developed a core belief that all money comes from

God and passes through other people, and that I must honor God in all that I do, my financial choices reflect those beliefs. This is very different from the old belief that many of us were taught early on—that money doesn't grow on trees.

When it comes to earning money, I have found that my efforts to achieve a financial goal must be of good service to others. If I act simply based on achieving more money, my motives are skewed and I will not be able to achieve or sustain the results for a long period, nor will I feel good about it, spiritually.

For example, when I took my first job in the auto industry, I set a 10-year career goal to become a Vice President of Quality. I shared this goal with my wife, parents, and some of my acquaintances. Speaking this aloud brought it to power and gave it life and momentum. My thoughts, feelings, and actions aligned with the goal, and I achieved Director of Quality in less than 10 years. Notice that I did not set a 10-year income goal. I set a goal that required me to be of service and the promotion would be the fruit of that service, as would the higher income from that increased responsibility.

Starting from a data entry clerk, the more I poured into learning and creating improvement ideas to serve others, the more financial success followed. In virtually every case, I was not seeking the next position or promotion; the opportunity was provided to me. Each year, the tree grew, the fruit grew, and the quality of the fruit improved. Our words have power.

Here's another example of a misguided saying.

"SAVE YOUR MONEY FOR A RAINY DAY."

This saying is self-fulfilling. While having enough money set aside for a "rainy day" is being responsible, be careful that you are not creating that rainy day by expecting it.

When I reflect on events in my life, I did not have this saying firmly planted. Yes, I thought saving money was important, but it was not at a level of priority that brought my ideas, emotions, and actions into alignment with saving money.

In our early years, we lived paycheck to paycheck and didn't have enough money to consider alternatives, nor did we treat money as a tool. The more money I made, the more we spent on our lifestyle.

If we had learned to invest our money first, the harvest from those investments would have given us more money. Plus, the seeds from the harvest could have been invested to earn even more money. Instead, as with most people, we tried to live on the fruit from a single tree and save some of the harvest for later, instead of planting some of the seeds and growing a bigger harvest.

These are just two of many examples of well-intended, but misguided advice.

The idea that words are powerful also has a more subtle meaning. Sometimes it's not what was said, but what was *not* said. As parents, most of our paradigms, beliefs, and values become duplicated into our children, what we do and do not know, our thoughts, ideas, and beliefs. In my case, I was never taught how to properly invest money, so I took the ready-fire-aim approach. I made uninformed decisions and hoped they would hit the target while relying on people that were not necessarily looking out for my best interests. Here is what it looked like.

Most of us make money, spend money, and repeat. I remember the first time I wanted to take some of our money and begin to save for our children's college and our retirement. We took our fruit, gave it to a financial planner we had met at church, and kept making deposits each month. The only problem was the stock market crashed. We lost any interest we had earned and some of the principal. It can take many years to get back to the same level you started when this occurs.

This same type of event has happened several times over my career. I have since learned that when I invest in a mutual fund or using an investment firm, I take all the risk. I am using 100% of my money and paying the fees for the funds directly or from within the fund. The managers of the fund don't have any financial risk.

How often does a financial manager or the managers of investment funds such as a 401(k) or similar fund look at your investments to make recommendations or choices that are best for you? I have found that when the market declines, my money declines, but the fees do not decline. Today, if I work with an investment advisor, I am looking for someone that gets paid only when my investment is successful. Therefore, their success is tied to my success. This provides a win-win solution. However, I do understand that I am still taking all the risks.

In 2008, we were building a new home. I had heard that if you build a home, you will never lose money. So, as we were building, several things were going over budget. First, my liquid capital was non-existent, but I wanted to get specific things done with the home. So, I decided to cash out 50% of my 401(k), taking a 10% penalty and paying taxes on what I withdrew. This was during the time of the automotive industry crash, immediately followed by the banking crisis. As it turned out, the 50% of the money I had left in the 401(k) lost 70% of its value in just a few weeks.

Everyone in my circle told me how foolish it was to take out my money early, that I should leave it in there for the future, for the "rainy day." As it turned out, I could get the house built to the level we desired and avoided most of the money being lost in the crash.

I was surely proud of my decision, boasting to others about what I had done. However, I had not yet fully learned my lesson. During the same time frame, the plant I was working in closed. I ended up taking an assignment that required me to relocate. The job was about a 2.5-hour drive from where we lived. The beautiful home we built on a pond, with a walkout finished basement leading to a plush yard and sandy beach, three miles from Lake Michigan, would not be where we were planted.

For 15 months, I stayed with friends, living in their basement while the rest of the family lived in the dream house. Not an optimal situation for the family. One of the lessons I missed here was the opportunity for me to begin developing another stream of income. Specifically, passive income. I found a home in the area where I was currently working and was able to purchase it while still owning the other home. There was a missed opportunity. I was speaking the words: *"So many people are selling their home on short sales to have huge debt written off. I should be able to do the same."*

I was trying to do what I thought everyone else was doing. I had met several people who had lost their job and were relocating to get another. Unfortunately, due to the declining market conditions, they were often left to sell their home for less than their mortgage, thus creating short sale conditions. When this occurred, the bank would write off the negative equity, and the person who had to sell their house was left with poor credit, significantly impacting their ability to buy their next home. But, of course, I had only been focused on the debt being forgiven, not the consequences that would accompany that decision.

A short sale felt dirty and wrong, but I was sure that this debt forgiveness would be what I deserved. After all, so many others were doing it. Financially, I was in a good position. I had a well-paying job and was able to buy the second home while owning the first, so I didn't need the short sale. But, based on what I had learned, it would have been smarter to operate the home as a rental property. My rent rate could have been at least the minimum amount to cover the mortgage—allowing the property value to appreciate without money out-of-pocket. My level of awareness at that time didn't allow me to see that opportunity, so I sold the home on a short sale.

I outsmarted myself. I had an equity line of credit on it. Because I bought a second home, this line of credit was simply attached to the new home I bought—no benefit of the short sale. In the end, I gave up the home, in which we had more than $350,000 invested, for a meager $225,000, of which only $7,350 was forgiven in the short sale from the primary mortgage. This harmed my personal credit for the next several years. The money I saved, so I thought, by taking it out of my 401(k) in the crash, was spent on selling my house. The equity that I should have had evaporated in a matter of months.

I realize now that there were two lessons for me here.
- First, there is a heavy emotional cost to following bad advice or making poor decisions, which can be draining and painful.
- Second, there is a significant financial cost to making investment decisions without proper guidance.

I hadn't saved money for a rainy day. My words, "that everyone else is doing it, so I should be able to," certainly came to fruition. Our words have power. They can create and destroy.

Things have since improved. Over the last three years, my perspective on money has become completely different from what I had learned early on. I tell my children not to participate in a 401(k) or retirement plan. Instead, use your money to create multiple streams of passive income. This will allow you to have the tools available to increase your service to others.

By planting more trees—multiple streams of passive income—over time, you can develop an orchard that keeps producing, fueling your ability to serve. If your heart is right, and you are doing things for the right reasons, each day will be filled with sunshine, and if it rains, you can enjoy it, not fear it. With the orchard, retirement will become much clearer. This point is evident in the following parable:

"One gives freely yet grows all the richer; another withholds what he should give, and only suffers want." —*Proverbs 11:24 ESV / 9*

Words are also powerful in another way. Everything you say, think, and feel is a prayer and command. Think about that because it is true. Whatever you give consistent energy and attention to is magnified. It doesn't mean everything that you think about becomes true but pay attention to what you speak because you are giving creative thought and energy to those words. One of the most impactful examples of this happened in March of 2021.

I was working a very well-paying job as an Assistant General Manager. I was second in command of an automotive electronics manufacturing plant. The plant had tremendous growth and success from 2011 through 2017. In 2018, significant financial impacts beyond my control dramatically affected my compensation. In addition, there were several upper-level management changes, which changed how we were able to run the division.

It was very frustrating for me. With each management change came another round of proving yourself, regardless of past results. In this last turn of management change, I could feel my motivation slipping away each day.

In the fall of 2019, I attended a conference with my wife for the company she was working with. She had found a great organization with superb products to help people with their nutrition—bridging the gap between what we eat and what we should eat to maintain or improve our nutrition. I didn't realize that this event would trigger a significant shift in our lives.

My plan for the conference was to stay at the hotel, swim in the pool, maybe work out, and be available for her during her breaks and go to dinner. I had no intentions of being an attendee of the conference. Thursday evening was free and open to the public, so I went with her. There were 10,000 people at this event. I didn't meet anyone that wasn't happy. I had been to my fair share of automotive conferences, and I had never seen this many happy people in one place. So, we bought a ticket for myself, and I attended the conference with her.

Throughout the conference, a seed was planted in my mind. I can remember the exact *aha* moment. Dr. Kenny Harless, who was to become my future mentor and close friend, explained the possibility of what this company had to offer and how I was trapped in my fear and misery working my current job. This could become the vehicle that could take me out of the automotive field and allow me to work alongside my wife. It would be a dream come true. Immediately, I could feel the thought, and my heart aligned with the idea.

In February of 2020, Laura signed up for a course called *Thinking into Results*, developed by Bob Proctor, and led by our mentor, Dr. Kenny Harless—his first time leading the course. Initially, I was not involved in what she was doing. Then the Covid-19 pandemic broke out in March 2020, forcing me to work from home. This was a blessing as I began to get involved in the program.

In December of 2020, I wrote the following goal:

I am so happy and grateful now that I am working alongside my wife, increasing our influence daily, building a world-class team that is five layers deep, and driving multiple streams of passive income providing $200,000 per month by December of 2021.

I began to say this goal aloud every morning. I wrote the goal every morning. I had the goal in my pocket every day. I even recorded it on a voice loop that I would listen to. I created a picture of what it would look like, and when I placed my hand in my pocket, it would trigger the picture.

I found that I had developed an emotional attachment to it in a relatively short time. My thoughts and my actions began to align with it. When I returned to the office in January of 2021, I sat down with my manager and told him that I would not be working in the same capacity by the end of the year. Instead, I would begin taking steps to ensure the team could move forward successfully without me. This is how sure I was it was going to happen.

I have also found that the Lord aligns our thoughts and desires. He wants us to have what we want.

Luke 11:9 says, "So I say to you, keep asking, and it will be given to you. Keep searching, and you will find. Keep knocking, and the door will be opened to you."

In November of 2020, we had a vacation opportunity come up with an invitation from a couple at our church asking us to go to Mexico with them the second week in February of 2021. The Lord planned this, as he knew what was in the future.

My job was becoming a mess. The new executive management was taking a different approach. The team was continually centralizing decision-making, taking control of what we were doing away from us. My manager and I had worked together for more than 20 years, with the freedom to run our divisions as we saw fit. We delivered consistent results with year-over-year improvements. However, over the past two years, significant issues had arisen that were not in our direct control and had significantly impacted financial results as our facility was responsible for more than 70% of the revenue for the entire group.

We had developed a team with almost a family concept. The new management thought we were too influential and had too much control. It was their perception, not reality. However, someone's perception is their reality.

In the last week of January 2021, the inevitable happened. My long-time business partner, my manager and friend, was walked out of the business. It's a shame how it was handled. A new manager was hired and was to start in a couple of weeks. I would be in charge until he arrived. This was painful to my ego as I felt slighted to not even discuss or be presented the opportunity to take on the role, yet I was expected to train this person who did not have an electronics background. So, I managed for the first week. Before the new leader came in, I discussed with my wife about not continuing. We agreed that I should ask for the same separation package given to my previous manager.

Monday morning, I called the VP of Manufacturing in Europe and left a message that we needed to talk. He called back. I explained that I could not find it in my heart to train the new leader and that I would like to have the severance package outlined in my contract. He needed time to discuss this with the executive leadership and asked me for the rest of the week. In the interim, the new leader arrived. I worked to get him acclimated to the team and organizational processes for the rest of that first week.

While I was awaiting my answer, I was scheduled to fly to Mexico. I got the call that Friday and was told that the organization would not honor my request, I was expected to stay on to train the new leader. With that, they promised delivery of a discretionary bonus.

During the week of vacation, I spent time with the Lord and discussed options with my wife and friends. By the end of the week, I was sure of my decision. I knew that, after receiving the promised bonus, I would resign, meaning no more paycheck and no benefits. I would begin to work alongside my wife, who was making $300 a month. On March 19, 2021, my words came to fruition.

"I am so happy and grateful now that I am working alongside my wife."

As of this writing, I have yet to achieve the financial or team depth, but we are well on our way to seeing progress beyond what I ever thought possible.

POWER OF WORDS EXERCISE

Since I believe so strongly in the power of words, here are a few quick exercises to help you apply this concept in your life.

CHANGE YOUR IDIOMS:

- Think of at least two sayings (idioms) that limit the way you think or make decisions. If you need help with some ideas, do an online search for "common idioms."
- Now, rephrase the idiom so that it gives you power and focus. For example, "Money doesn't buy happiness" can be rephrased to "Money gives me choices and time freedom." Since money was never intended to buy happiness, the idiom misleads people to believe that money is not important, or that you have to choose between money and happiness, but you can't have both, which is not true.
- Use the power of words to energize your goals. If you do not have goals, you can still do this exercise.

ESTABLISH GOALS:

- Create a handwritten list of up to 300 goals you would love to accomplish. Big or small, write them down. My guess is you will start to struggle between 30 and 75 because most people have stopped dreaming and don't believe in themselves to think big.
- Be specific. Paint a detailed picture in your mind of each goal. When your list is complete, determine what is most important to you. If you're married, do the exercise individually for your personal goals, and then again together and create marriage goals. Agree on what is most important.
- Write them on index cards that you can carry and read them often as a reminder throughout the day.
- Over time, as you consistently speak your goals into reality with emotional charge, they will become your reality.

PRAY OUT LOUD:

When praying, do so out loud with specific intent. Speak the words you want God to hear. My prayers were very general in the past, including things like good health, financial freedom, and peace.

Be specific. I have found being specific is helpful. Here's two examples.

1.) When I am praying for something to do with my health or someone else's, I ask God specifically:

"Lord, remove the blockage in my heart and heal her broken rib."

2.) I once prayed to have more time to spend with my family. So, when I was let go from a job at the beginning of the summer, my prayer was answered. However, what I said and what I wanted weren't completely aligned. I wanted to have more time with my family, but I just left out that I wanted it with a continuous flow of income that would also allow me to accomplish the Lord's plans for my life.

My prayers take a little longer because they have more specific detail. However, when they are answered, the detail, clarity, and specifics let me know He is working all things for my good.

***

To take a deeper dive into goal setting, I recommend you sign up for the *Thinking into Results* workshop. I have a link provided for you at the end of this book.

Schedule a discussion and commit to taking the course. It can change your life by providing you with the tools to understand that you can do anything you want to do; that your words will drive your actions which will provide you the results.

4th Lesson

FAITH OVER FEAR

• • •

Both faith and fear may sail into your harbor,
but only allow faith to drop anchor.
— Bear Grylls

What is more prominent in your life—faith or fear?

If it is fear, what has it cost you? Happiness, health, opportunity? Peace of mind? Love? Closeness to God? How much longer do you want to miss out on the many gifts of life awaiting you on the other side of fear?

If not fear, then faith? How strong is your faith—in yourself and God? Do you see God as something far away that you are trying to get close to, or have you discovered the closeness of God within your heart and mind?

But what is faith, and what is fear?

Fear is a feeling of discomfort with uncertainty and the unknown. It is using your most powerful tool, your imagination, to focus on and visualize an unpleasant result. It is *feeling* an outcome that you don't want as if it already happened. Some call it having negative expectations and negative creation.

Faith, on the other hand, has positive expectations. You believe something good will happen even if the evidence is not yet visible. That belief can be based on knowing and believing in your skills and abilities or your belief that there is a higher power—God—that can make things happen regardless of current circumstances. Faith does not have to be blind leaps. The more you believe in yourself and God, the easier it is to make those challenging choices.

So many times, unknowingly, I have chosen faith over fear. When doing so, things had always blossomed when I was in alignment with that inner voice—the Holy Spirit. There were many times that I allowed fear to carry my decisions, and when I did, I found that I had chosen tiptoeing safely through life on a path to death.

For me, fear and faith are not just words; they convey meaning.

FEAR

F — False

E — Evidence or Emotion

A — Appearing

R — Real

FAITH

F — Forever

A — Always

I – Inevitably

T — Trusting

H — Him

REFLECT AND MOVE FORWARD

• • •

"Your behavior is causing your results…and your conditioning is causing your behavior."
— *Bob Proctor*

Fear affects everyone. If we allow it, it can hold us back and stop us from accomplishing all that we have the potential to do; even blocking our mental, emotional, and spiritual intimacy with God

While writing this book and thinking about many of my different life events leading up to this writing, many of those memories have shown me the extent to which fear has affected my choices and decisions.

Not only do I see it in myself, but my fears have affected Laura as well. She has taken on many of my fear-based cues of uncertainty and carried the struggles of health, finances, or family. I see it in my children today as they emulate the fear-based actions and words I have spoken into them through the years. It is amazing how much control we can allow fear to carry.

Most of the associates I have worked with over the years have been stuck in the hamster wheel of life and have allowed fear to drive their decisions. Our shop-talk conversations included how they are not satisfied with their job, pay, boss, family situation, and where they live. Yet, they continue to do the same thing each day in hopes of getting to the point of making enough money to be able to retire. Does any of this sound familiar to you? If yes, ask yourself this question:

Are you letting fear hold you back or is it driving your decision to make necessary but uncomfortable changes?

There was a point when I had shared many of the same feelings and frustrations as my coworkers. Just like them, I had felt as though I were on the hamster wheel of life, traveling a safe path on my way to the end of my life—my death.

The harsh reality is that we only have one chance at life with no do-overs, but I was making decisions as if life would go on forever. When I allowed fear to steer my path and limit my actions, it was as if it was no big deal to waste time by living in fear and avoiding important decisions. Ultimately, I had learned that allowing fear to be greater than my faith, allowed stifling a multitude of possibilities in my life.

There were career changes or advancement opportunities present-ed to me. I can recall that nervous feeling; the butterflies start go-ing, and excitement builds around the potential of a change. Is it an opportunity to improve? Is the grass greener there, or am I already where I need to be? Isn't this a question most of us ask ourselves when these things come up?

Being my own barrier against moving forward, I let fear and anx-iety pull me back. I chose to stay with what I know, the comfort, the easier road to travel. Leaving myself working safely with the situation that I know, regardless of whether I am happy or satisfied, it is safe. Looking back, it was tiring being on that hamster wheel—so much energy devoted to being safe.

Take a few moments to reflect upon how you make decisions and the outcomes in your life and see if you can discover if your decisions are mainly based on fear or faith.

Here are a couple of examples to help explain how I allowed fear or safety to direct my path. Maybe you can relate.

When Laura and I chose to re-enlist in the Army back in 1987 for another three years, we could have let faith guide our decision by re-enlisting without arranging our next assignment. In doing so, we could have been stationed anywhere. Who knows what opportunity or new friends would be there awaiting? Fear drove our decision. In effect, by doing things our way, we ignored God and the blessings He had in store for us.

We weren't sure if we could make it outside of the Army as a mar-ried couple, as we had never tried it, so, we chose to re-enlist. But we also had more plans. I contacted the base we were previously assigned to and worked a deal with the recruiting team that would allow us to return to the base we left in Georgia, working at the same dining facility. A familiar place, safe, allowing fear to persevere over faith.

In another opportunity for change, after Laura and I left the military in early 1990, I took my first job as a contract employee working for one of the big three auto companies. I wasn't going to take the job initially. The offer was good, but I would make more money collecting unemployment. Funny, my father-in-law didn't see it that way, so after a few one-way discussions, my viewpoint changed. Out of fear of finding my own place to live without a job (a main point of the one-way discussion), in a short time I took the job.

In 1992, I found myself standing in a pile of drywall from a kitchen renovation that I was doing because I was out of work. In that same moment we decided to accept a job that would see us relocate to Sheboygan, Wisconsin.

On the surface, it seemed like a decision based on faith as we had to relocate to an area we knew nothing about, working with people we didn't know, and having no family support near us. The facts were that my contract job was eliminated, I was again on unemployment, and I had no other job offers. My choices were to take the job or have faith that the right job would come that didn't require us to sell our house and relocate the family. We chose the logical and safe option to accept the new position and move.

In 1999, an opportunity came up to take a new position with a new company. The position itself was a lateral transfer, meaning no real change in responsibility, and there wasn't much of a change in pay.

I had started looking for another job out of fear that my position would be eliminated even though I had provided consistently positive results with the projects that I had been a part of since I began working there. My reputation and results were good. I was moving forward and taking on more responsibility over time. But I had experienced the effects of the company going through growing pains. I saw multiple structure changes, some of which directly impacted what I was doing and to who I was reporting. There was a rumor among the employees that it was on the brink of bankruptcy. So, Laura and I chose to move to a new company. After all, the grass had to be greener there. Again, a safe choice.

Today, I live with the understanding that we have a small rear-view mirror. We only look back to learn and to understand what drove us to make the decisions we did at the time. We cannot change the past. We can only reflect and move forward. That's not to say I haven't occasionally found myself wondering where I would have been and what would have happened if I had chosen to stay in any one of those previous companies. Where would I be?

Yes, we have always been willing to try new things during our many moves, but, when I look back, we made those decisions to move based on what we perceived as a necessity rather than what we truly wanted.

Each of our decisions seemed to come with the promise of a job on the other side—of knowing that I could afford a new home mortgage. Only two of our more than 16 moves had an unknown future.

The first unknown was ending our military career in the U.S. Army and relocating back to Michigan as civilians. We had no plan or direction, only knowing that we did not want to re-enlist in the Army for another four years. If we had re-enlisted, it would mean nine years of service completed, which is nearly halfway of what is needed for retirement. We felt doing this would place us on a road that would have kept us in the military for at least 20 years. We wanted a different life for our family. We wanted to be close to our parents and siblings. Only through faith were we going to have a path forward provided.

When we returned, we moved in with Laura's parents and her younger sister still living at home. They graciously allowed us to move in with them. There were three of us now. Our firstborn son was about six months old. It was a busy home, but we all made it work. I had no idea what we would do as I had not yet graduated from college. I was a cook in the Army, so those skills created the opportunity for an entry-level position in restaurants. To make it on our own with a family would be difficult at my level of pay. It was a fearful situation.

Early on, I spent time teaching myself how to use word processing programs. This was still relatively new in 1990, and it wasn't common for everyone to have this type of working knowledge. By learning it, I thought it might give me an advantage over others when interviewing for a job. We had applied for unemployment, and I was searching for a job that would provide enough money to give us a chance to live independently. Looking back, I see that God's hand and guidance were in everything.

Through the unemployment office, I would be helped with resume building, interviewing, and training opportunities. I was offered an opportunity to meet with a temporary employment agency early on. This agency had a few clerical openings. I reluctantly went because it was a requirement of unemployment. When I showed up, they gave me a typing test. My high school typing class paid off as did my self-taught word processing skills. I was not a fast typist, but I was accurate.

Within a week, the agency offered me an opportunity to work for them at one of the big three automotive companies on a full-time, long-term assignment. The pay wasn't great, but better than I could have made being a cook at a nearby restaurant.

Initially, I was going to turn the job down because the pay wasn't ideal. but my father-in-law wisely convinced me otherwise. This decision turned into a 30-year career in the automotive industry. We didn't know it at the time; however, by choosing faith over fear, I was placed on a path that would provide many years of ever-increasing income and opportunity for Laura and me.

It wasn't an easy situation. As I worked that job, I also delivered pizza on the weekends, and attended college part-time trying to complete my degree. While I did that, Laura focused on caring for the family during the day. She would waitress most nights and weekends. Her parents were a huge help juggling our schedules to ensure there was always someone to be with our son. Within six months, Laura and I were able to qualify for a mortgage, thanks to the VA, and purchased our first home.

I thank the Lord for providing this window of opportunity and motivating my father-in-law to provide the convincing I needed to take the position. The Lord does provide us with free will, and I could have stayed in the realm of fear but fortunately chose faith.

The Bible gives us great guidance surrounding fear. Below are a few verses that I have grown to love:

Isaiah 41:10 - Fear not, for I am with you; be not dismayed, for I am your God; I will strengthen you, I will help you, I will uphold you with my righteous right hand.

2 Timothy 1:7 - For God gave us a spirit not of fear but power and love and self-control.

1 John 4:18 - There is no fear in love, but perfect love casts out fear. For fear has to do with punishment, and whoever fears has not been perfected in love.

The second unknown future came in March of 2021, when I left my corporate career to pursue the dream of working alongside Laura.

Who voluntarily gives up a six-figure income with a top-tier company after 16 years? Especially without another equal or better opportunity of pay and benefits already lined up.

When Laura and I came to a final agreement that I would officially turn in my notice ending my 30-year automotive career, there was immense fear for both of us, but it wasn't enough to stop us. We understood the power of faith and the law of cause and effect. This next stage of our life was a leap toward freedom, knowing that we had to sow new seeds, focus on larger goals, and be intentional with our faith.

FROM RESIGNATION TO FREEDOM

*It is not always what we know or analyzed before we
make a decision that makes it a great decision. It is
what we do after we make the decision to implement
and execute it that makes it a good decision.*
—*William Pollard*

Taking the leap of faith from resignation to freedom was an enormous endeavor. Our final decision to do so was encouraged by Matthew 7:7-8.

"Ask, and it will be given to you; seek and you will find; knock, and the door will be opened to you. 8 For everyone who asks receives; the one who seeks finds; and to the one who knocks, the door will be opened."

Laura and I were asking, seeking, and knocking but weren't expecting things to rush in so quickly. By year-end there would be a quick and aggressive change. The mess that had consumed the company I was working for fueled my determination to do something different. I set my sights to work alongside Laura by December of 2021.

Being in a mess and receiving a paycheck versus voluntarily jumping out, without the certainty of benefits and a paycheck, brings a level of fear and anxiety that neither of us had ever experienced before.

First, I want to say thank you to Laura who was incredibly supportive in the process. I know she did not want me to quit the job. After all, I had a great title, a great team, a great track record, great benefits, a great vacation policy, and excellent pay. We had just finished building a new house, and our youngest son was living with us, attending college, and working. What wife wants to see this type of security removed?

The Lord was opening doors and sending so many signs our way to indicate His intent to fulfill our desires. It is simply amazing to see how He works. I have found His plan puts you in a position that ensures when you jump, you are jumping through faith. Faith is risk, and our taking action will drive us towards the opportunity He has provided for us.

My boss being let go and my not being considered to take over his position provided motivation to act. Additionally, upper management brought more restrictions, further reducing my ability to operate with the level of freedom that I desired—increasing my frustration.

Laura's excitement around the idea of what could be versus my current misery drove her to provide agreement and support, if only outwardly for what I wanted to do. This was magnified by her love for me and her trust in God.

I assume she thought I was going through a mid-life crisis, or maybe I was turning a bit crazy? I am sure she shed many tears privately over the situation. We had spent several weeks talking about it and having conversations with the Lord. The entire situation must have just seemed surreal to her. But, on the day that I needed her agreement, she was there for me, supportive, saying that if I were sure this is what I wanted to do, she would be on board. So, she put her faith in God and me that things would work out—and they did.

Maybe I was a bit crazy? I had spent many hours in prayer, listening to God, asking whether what I was about to do was part of his plan for me. After all, we were still in what people were calling a pandemic. The world economy was suffering immensely because of all the government shutdowns, and many people were feeding off fear.

So many new things have shown up in our lives over the past few years; new people, new ideas of how to create income, and a deeper relationship with Jesus.

People who have known me for a long time, that I had worked with for years, would have told you that there is no way he did that. I was growing, and I was hungry for something new. God opened my mind and heart to new possibilities. I was looking for a new way to make a difference.

In preparation for my resignation, I had written several versions of the letter that would inform the company of my intention. I would read what I had written, reflect, and seek guidance from both people close to me and from God. Ultimately, in the final version, I had eliminated any reference to bitterness that I had felt and replaced it with gratitude, leaving the door open by offering my future assistance as the company would see fit. After all, it was not the company's fault that I was driven to this decision point. They had wanted me to stay. I had asked to be provided a severance as outlined in my contract, but they insisted that I stay, even offering a discretionary bonus as a sign of their commitment.

When I finally decided to resign, it was the most amazing thing. It was as if an 800-pound weight had fallen off my shoulders. My demeanor instantly changed regarding the office, my team, and family. There was a sense of peace, joy, and confidence. I knew that my future was no longer going to be in my control, that I was turning it over to God, ensuring that my plans were His plans. I was choosing faith over fear. It was about another week before I officially delivered my resignation, and on March 19th, 2021, this phase of my life was over, and a new phase was born.

When Laura and I began to write this book, it had been more than one year since my great resignation. I want to tell you that it has been a year of jubilation—happier and healthier than I have been in years. Financially, I am blessed beyond what I thought possible. More doors opened than I could have ever imagined. So often, people miss the opportunity to experience what is on the other side of fear. I am so happy and grateful that Laura and I chose faith—allowing us to do so.

If you are stuck in what you are doing and don't see a way out, ask yourself this question:

Am I letting fear drive my decisions?

My experience says anything is possible when we choose faith over fear. Faith is not just believing. Faith is acting on what you believe. One thing is for sure; if you aren't willing to put faith over fear, you may never discover the many blessings that await you.

Be bold, be courageous, confident, focused, and choose faith; you will be glad you did.

6th Lesson

KNOWING — DOING GAP

• • •

"Inaction breeds doubt and fear. Action breeds
confidence and courage. If you want to conquer fear, do
not sit home and think about it. Go out and get busy."
—Dale Carnegie

Many times, in my past, I found myself knowing the right thing to do but not doing it. Have you ever found yourself in this type of situation? You know what you should do, but, for whatever reason, you chose not to do it? I have discovered that this form of avoidance is known as the Knowing-Doing Gap.

I know what to do, but consciously or unconsciously, I choose not to do it.

For example, I know that eating dairy is not good for my heart and that, over time, it builds up plaque in my bloodstream that can lead to bad things. However, as I pass by that ice cream shop on that hot summer day, I choose to order a triple scoop. Have you ever been there? I know what foods I should eat to be healthy. Unless I consciously choose to eat those health-conscious foods and turn the choice into a habit, I will likely continue to struggle with the knowing and doing gap.

I see how this gap has existed in many parts of my life. So many times, I have seen my weight fluctuate up and down by over 25 pounds. I have done the Atkin's diet and lost 25 pounds. However, I didn't change my habits or lifestyle and put the weight back on in less than six months.

I have done the HGT diet, giving myself shots, again losing 25 pounds and gaining it back in about the same amount of time. I joined the gym, and worked out five days a week, on several occasions over the years, each time losing weight, but only to return to where I had been previously. Not to mention Weight Watchers, paleo diet, Mediterranean diet, and I am sure there were a few more. All to only see me revert to somewhere near where I was before. In some cases, worse than before.

Does any of this sound familiar to you?

Let's look at the work-life balance we always hear people talk about. Over the years, there have been several times that I knew (and Laura knew) that I should slow down, work fewer hours, or suffer the consequences of illness or burnout. My priorities were flawed. I placed work above God, my family, and myself. Due to the stress, I developed things like Crohn's disease, diverticulitis, spinal meningitis, and prostate cancer. I even had my appendix removed. My only stopper seemed to be the hospital.

There were so many opportunities for me to stop working and be home on time for dinner, yet I chose to stay at work instead. So many commitments that I had made to spend time with people, whether personal or professional, only to cancel my commitment. The knowing-doing gap for me was rather large.

So, what are some ways that we can work to close the gap? Sometimes, through the largest problems, the greatest breakthroughs emerge. The pandemic, for me, turned out to be a significant blessing. During that time, not only did I become aware of this thing called the knowing-doing gap, but I also learned how to work on closing gaps that existed in many areas of my life. I have learned that if we increase our self-awareness of what causes the gap for us, we can begin to work to reduce the gap.

One example is realizing that I like to eat when I am placed in a high-stress situation. Unless I find a way to reduce the stress or develop a healthier mindset, dieting would continue to place me in this never-ending battle with my weight. If I were to choose not to do the diet and not to exercise but continue eating as a reaction to stress, I would just simply continue to get heavier.

Now, when I find myself in a high-stress situation and start eating, I ask myself if I'm eating because of hunger or stress. Just having this awareness has reduced the knowing-doing gap for me. This small shift allowed my wife and I to use the pandemic as an opportunity to become healthier and in better shape than we have been in years. So far, we have been able to maintain and continue improving ourselves through understanding this.

Sometimes the fear of failure stops us. I have learned that action is important. I am enjoying the opportunity of establishing goals and using the pursuit of those goals to close the knowing-doing gap in many parts of my life.

Over the past year, I have focused on improving myself. This includes a morning routine of waking up around 5 a.m., five days a week (6 a.m. on Saturday and Sunday) and completing a daily Bible verse for the daily devotional with Laura before getting out of bed. Then, I drink a full glass of water, brew a pot of coffee, and read scripture. After reading scripture, I spend one hour on self-improvement. This includes reading, listening to podcasts, writing my goals, and working on a plan to help achieve my goal. Then I exercise and eat.

Trust me; there are days I don't want to do this. However, I have learned that maintaining a routine is important to keep things going. Making an excuse for why I shouldn't or can't is easy. There have been times when I let those excuses win. I now work with belief that, if I feel like I don't want to do something that is important, then I should do it and act immediately.

Where many people fail is convincing themselves, I haven't done this in a week. Why start over? By not looking at this as a failure but as an opportunity to start fresh, you can give yourself another chance.

An acquaintance of mine, Jim Packard, was co-author of a book titled The Consistency Chain for Network Marketing. This book shares the simple process of using a calendar and placing an X on the date you complete the activity you desire, creating a chain of consistency. It is like a visual scorecard for yourself. If you miss a day, there is a blank box. However, you can fill the box the next day, starting again. Through determination and understanding that if I choose to do these things, I will be moving toward where I want to be.

1. What areas of your life do you have a Knowing-Doing Gap?
2. What can you do to shrink the gap?
3. Do you have a daily routine that includes doing something for yourself?

I recommend creating one. It doesn't have to be hours long. It can be your first 15 or 30 minutes of the morning. Doing something for the Lord first, then yourself, may help set the tone for what you do the rest of the day.

YOUR PERCEPTION IS YOUR TRUTH

• • •

"It's not who you are that holds you back,
it's who you think you're not."
— Denis Waitley

Have you ever been so convinced of something that you found yourself swearing it to be absolute truth—only to later be shown or proven that what you believed to be true wasn't?

One day I was setting up a volleyball net for a party we were having at our house. When I got everything out, there were no stakes for the ropes. I was convinced my youngest son, Jason, had used the set with his youth group, and they didn't return it with the stakes. I was so sure this was what happened that when I was through discussing it with him, he agreed and offered me an apology. He went to the store to buy some new stakes for me. I set it up for the party when he returned. Funny though, several months later, I was moving some of the Christmas stuff I had left in the garage. There, lying in a pile of lights, were the stakes from the volleyball net. I had taken them out trying to set up some lights and ended up not using them. But, of course, I didn't share this with Jason. (If you are reading this, sorry about that, Son.)

I have found that our perception is our truth, but not necessarily the truth. Our perception is based upon events that have been a part of our past, from which we develop future beliefs and expectations. Why then did I say that Jason didn't return the tent stakes? It's simple. He had not returned things numerous times after using them, so I allowed his past behavior to determine my assumption that it was him.

"Past proves future."

Oddly enough, knowing that he had not returned things previously, I convinced him that I was right. What teenager would have bought replacement tent stakes without being provided money or receiving something beneficial for them, had they not believed they had made a mistake?

I have learned that many of the truths or perceptions that I carry regarding a past event or situation are nothing more than habitual mental assumptions from past experiences, but it doesn't have to be that way.

You're not stuck in a set of beliefs unless you choose to be. Whatever perceptions and beliefs you hold true can be altered and updated by expanding your awareness, knowledge, or belief about that situation. You simply have to be willing to ask different questions and look at things differently. This can be tricky if you have a lot of pride and a strong need to be right, but if not, then a willingness to look at things differently creates more options for you and your life.

A common mistake that many people make when talking with someone is to assume that the person they are speaking with has similar beliefs to themselves. For example, when looking at my life, I learned that when engaged in a conversation with someone else, what they say, how they say it, what they believe, and any choices or actions they take are based on their truth and perception. A person can be factually inaccurate with what they say, but in their mind, it is true because it is based on their perception.

How you perceive things matters more than what you are looking at or thinking about. True or not, your beliefs are based on your perception. Change your perception, and you will see things differently.

I remember a significant event that forever changed my perception regarding our ability to be physically healed by God.

I had heard stories of people seeing miraculous healings. People being able to walk again, limbs growing, cancer being cured, overcoming drug addiction instantly—to name a few. When I heard about these types of things in the past, I had not yet seen them, and with my upbringing, I was reluctant to accept that such things could truly happen. When I did witness a miraculous healing, like someone getting up out of a wheelchair or stop using a walker, I would give it no credence and think that it was their adrenaline from the situation. In the back of my mind, I would wonder—will they still be changed later?

I don't know where your beliefs are on this topic. I know several religions believe it's not possible and that it only occurred during the time of Jesus. Others may not believe it to be possible at all.

Several years ago, I found myself in a Charismatic Catholic Church outside of Ann Arbor, Michigan. I was attending a healing service led by an evangelist who was visiting from Australia. My wife had heard of it through a family member. We both had some health issues between the two of us, so she insisted we go. It was an interesting service. There appeared to be people who were being healed from their ailments, but doubts would seep into my mind about whether it was true or not.

At the time, I was suffering from plantar fasciitis. This is an extremely painful condition where there is inflammation of the band of tissue (ligament) that connects the heel bone to the toes (plantar fascia), causing excruciating pain in the heel. It can lead to ligament tearing. My custom arch supports helped a little bit to reduce the pain, but I had been suffering for many months.

During the service, I was in prayer with my hands on the gentleman next to me, praying for healing in his shoulder. As I was praying, a tremendous heat came into my foot and ankle. I thought that it was strange. When the heat disappeared, so did the pain in my foot. I thought, no way, was this healing stuff real? I kept this to myself. After all, what if the pain were to come back? Then I would not have truly been healed.

After the service, my family went home. The next day, I woke up with no pain. I went to work—no pain. When I came home, I told my wife that I wanted to run today. I went on a short run and had no pain. That evening I shared with her that God had healed my foot during the service. The pain never returned. I have run hundreds of miles since the healing.

I now use that event as a testimony to others, explaining the Glory of God and His love for us. My truth, my perception, was forever altered because of what I experienced. The Lord is constantly providing opportunities for me to believe. He gave me hard physical evidence to prove that He exists. He has written in scripture:

Then Jesus told him: "You believe because you have seen me. Blessed are those who believe without seeing me." (John 20:29 NLT)

For we live by faith, not by sight. (2 Corinthians 5:7 NIV)

Now faith is confidence in what we hope for and assurance about what we do not see. (Hebrews 11:1)

Ultimately, this experience has been a critical element in transforming how I react to what someone may say or do that isn't in alignment with my thinking. In the past, when I didn't agree with someone's viewpoint, whether it was political, spiritual, financial, or something else, I would find myself arguing and providing all the evidence as to why I was right, and they weren't. I would get upset when they didn't understand or wouldn't agree, even with facts to prove my point.

Now, I understand that the person is coming from their perception. They haven't had the same experiences, so how can I expect them to see or believe the same way as me?

Through this eye-opening shift in my awareness, I have identified a simple strategy for being mindful of other people's perceptions.

When someone is upset or even yelling at me, I make an effort not to react. In my mind, I ask myself, what is their truth? What is driving this behavior? Is there something that I should have communicated? Taking the few seconds to run these thoughts in my head provides a delay to what used to be a trigger to fight back.

Today, it is rare that I find myself in confrontational situations. But when I do, most often, when I catch myself in my old pattern of reacting, I apologize, asking what actions or words I used to upset them and is there something I can do to help?

When someone has an entirely different view of a situation, listening carefully to understand what may be driving their point of view helps. Then, when appropriate, I provide an open-ended question that aligns with what they have spoken about.

Here's an example of an open-ended question.

"What is most important to you right now?"

Have you ever found yourself in a situation where you knew the other person you were speaking with had such a difference in their views that you were sure they would not listen to you?

I have found that before engaging in a conversation with someone who holds an opinion or expectation different than mine, to reduce their defenses and allow for a constructive discussion, I walk myself through what I want to say to create a picture that I care about what they think.

Finally, if I continue to find myself engaged with a person or group that isn't willing to be open to listening or understanding questions, I engage with them less often.

Sometimes people's beliefs are so strong that I may not be able to create an understanding with them that offers an opportunity for genuine discussion. To continually maintain my awareness of those whom I come in contact with, I use the following statement:

"I am so happy and grateful now that my mind is open to new possibilities daily. My old paradigms are quickly and easily changed based on the new levels of awareness that come to me with ease and enjoyment. Thank you, Lord."

Understanding that your perception is your truth opens new doors in all areas of your life. When you realize, as I did, that perception is a choice, then you will never be limited in your faith and belief because anything is possible when you believe it in your heart and mind. Choose to see all possibilities. Choose to believe that there is always another way to look at life differently.

The stories I have shared have been a testimony to the benefit of being flexible in your beliefs. When you willingly change your perception, you are changing the next chapter in the story of your life.

You do not have to be limited to the way things appear. Each time you open your mind and expand your perception, you create a new doorway for God to enter your life and shower you with blessings.

EPILOGUE

As I sit down and write the Epilogue, I am amazed at how much our lives have changed since Laura and I first met. It has been an incredible journey, and I have only shared the highlights of some important events that shaped our faith and our relationship.

In the beginning I introduced the five core life lessons that have had the most significant impact on our lives:

- ✓ Mindset is everything
- ✓ Happiness is a choice
- ✓ Faith over fear
- ✓ Our words are powerful
- ✓ Your truth is your perception

I shared these because they are the nuts and bolts of what I believe it takes to live a whole life. Nothing in life works if you don't have your mindset in proper order. If you are committed to personal and spiritual growth and are not happy with the direction of your life, then take a close look at your thoughts and beliefs. You may just need to do some housecleaning.

It's difficult to consolidate a lifetime of ideas and awareness into a few chapters of a book. The most important takeaway is that no matter what happens to you in life, you have to accept responsibility for your entire life experience. It's not easy, but it's worth it.

There is no doubt in my mind that Jesus Unleased My Potential (J.U.M.P.). My entire life has been a testimony of struggle, faith, and belief. If you feel a bit like I described in the introduction, someone who is on the hamster wheel of life, maybe it's time for you to allow Jesus to unleash your potential, too.

It has taken many more years than I wish it would have to be where Laura and I are today in our relationship with each other, Jesus, and our understanding of how to care for our mind, body, and spirit. What I do know is that as long as you are alive, it is never too late to give yourself, your partner, and God, a fresh start.

If you are ready to J.U.M.P, find a church that resonates with your spirit and take the leap of faith into God's arms. You'll be glad that you did.

Thank you, Jesus for the opportunity to glorify you through this book, and for the gift of my beautiful bride.

Amen.

OUR FINAL THOUGHTS

Now that you have read our stories, we have something fun to share. During our 6+ months of working on our material, we did not read each other's content or share any ideas. We were committed to writing a book together and wanted each of our stories to be our authentic thoughts, lessons, and memories from our 36+ years together without influencing each other's words. As we each wrote our parts separately, we had no way of knowing that we were both writing about Jesus unleashing our potential.

When we first started writing this book, we had a very different vision in mind. We had initially wanted to write about how we jumped from corporate America to where we are now, working together from home, and how you could do it, too. But the book took on a life of its own. Instead of focusing on how to change careers, it became a testimony to our faith and an opportunity for us to glorify Jesus.

Initially, our vision for the book title was *Jump*, but that title had already been used for many other books. So, we were advised to think of something unique that would stand out. Then, one day, God gave Laura the title while in the shower:

J.U.M.P. | Jesus Unleashed My Potential

It was the same but different. Now it was relevant. It had meaning to us and was perfect because our lives have been one J.U.M.P. after another, always leaping with our faith in God.

The reality is that early on in our lives, we did not know our potential or where we would end up. But, over the years, by pressing forward with faith, learning from our mistakes, and being dutiful to God's word, we can now see how God's hand was always in our lives.

Now, the word J.U.M.P. has a whole new meaning. When we say J.U.M.P. to ourselves or someone else, we're saying that God is always there, waiting for us to step up and step into His world. God is always there to help us reach our potential. Still, we must be willing to do the work, go through personal development, take risks, be faithful, and mature mentally, emotionally, and spiritually.

So how did we J.U.M.P.? It was first and foremost having a relationship with Jesus and going from glory to glory. Without Jesus, none of this would be possible—our 36-year marriage, our finances, our spiritual growth, and even our foundation.

We have to mention that the way this book came about is all God's plan and is yet another testimony to our faith. Years ago, while on a mission trip to the Dominican Republic, Steve was told (prophesized over) that he would write a book. Fast forward to 2021, when we happened to be in Las Vegas at a conference where we met David Strauss, one of the speakers (as well as author and writing coach) who would help us write this book.

When we sat at the restaurant for lunch, David was across from us, and we had no idea he was an author. But we started to talk, and well, the rest is history. God has always placed the right people in our path at the right time. We hope that each of us recognizes the gifts when they come, embraces them, and moves forward.

There is a lot that you can take away from this book, depending on what you believe and where you are in your life's journey. We want you to understand that there are decisions you can make to change your world completely. The most important decision, we believe, is the choice to allow Jesus to unleash your potential, too.

Our encouragement to anyone reading this book that wants positive change would be to know and have a relationship with Jesus.

If you don't know how to do that, let me lead you in a simple prayer that will give you that peace.

Lord Jesus, I confess my sins and ask for your forgiveness.

I believe that you died for my sins.

I want a relationship with you, and I want to make you my Lord and Savior.

Come into my heart and make me new. Thank you for loving me.

In Jesus name, Amen.

Of course, this is simply an example. You can ask Jesus to come into your heart in your own words. He loves you and wants a relationship with you.

A few final takeaways...

Having coaches and mentors made a big difference in our lives. We suggest you think seriously about getting a coach/mentor in the areas you want to improve the most, and hopefully, there are many areas. Growth and improvement are pivotal for a happy life. Don't worry about the cost. First, make the decision and commitment, and then you will find a way to make it happen. Then, invest in yourself, and the results will be amazing.

Being open-minded is what allows us to learn and grow. We have found that being open to possibilities and different ways of doing things have opened doors for us that we never even knew were there. Unfortunately, too many people are "stuck in their ways" and not open to things they do not yet understand. They are held back by comfort, fear, or the discomfort of uncertainty. We hope that through the examples in our stories, you will have the courage to be different, to be okay with making uncomfortable decisions, and decide to try something new.

Speaking of decisions, that is where everything happens—when you make a decision. Had Steve not decided to leave his corporate job, or had I not decided to do network marketing, we would still be on the hamster wheel of life. Today we are free. Free to serve others and make a difference.

We are making a difference with this book, our nutrition company, and our mindset coaching. It is our hope and prayer that the words we shared in our stories have inspired you to J.U.M.P. and have made a difference in your life, too.

"If you can believe, all things are possible to him who believes."
Mark 9:23

God Bless!

ACKNOWLEDGEMENTS

We want to thank Jesus, our Lord and Savior, for the journey because, without Him, none of this would be possible. We are grateful for the hills and valleys that have allowed us to become who we are today.

Life is a journey that cannot be accomplished alone. As we connect the dots looking back at the many seasons of life thus far, hundreds, if not thousands, of people have been a part of our journey and touched our lives along the way or have been touched by us.

Thank you to the following people for helping to make this book possible and for the many friends and family who have played an important role in our lives.

It would simply not be possible to mention every person that has made an impact on us. We are forever grateful—whether it was for a short moment or many years of friendship. Without them, we wouldn't be where we are today.

We thought it appropriate to share our gratitude for some that have touched our lives to show you the significance of whom God puts into our path.

First, thank you to David Strauss, who turned our vision of a book into reality. The 2021 event where we met is still providing many new paths of friendships and business opportunities. It is amazing how one decision can have such a profound impact on one's future. We could have said no to the conference. Without it, this book would not have been written, as we would not have met David Strauss. We are more than thankful for his teamwork in helping us put this together. Without him, our idea of writing a book would likely still be an idea. Thank you, David, for believing in us and making it a reality.

Our family played a significant role in developing and defining who we are. We are grateful for the opportunities that, through their thoughts, prayers, action, and guidance, helped shape our journey.

Thank you to our parents, Tom & Arlene Frederick, Robert & Nancy Allmen, and Janie Burson, who brought us into the world. A special thank you to Tom Frederick, Laura's dad, who instilled the gift of generosity and the glass being half full into our lives. His wisdom, love, and positive attitude have definitely impacted us.

Thank you to our children, Anthony, Olivia, and Jason. We love each of you and will continue to watch you achieve your goals and, where possible, provide our guidance to help you get there. Moving so many times probably wasn't easy, but you never complained. You have watched us do seemingly crazy things, yet we stand united. Thank you!

We are grateful to Jeff Gary, who Steve met in 1999, a man he would later work for and learn from for 20+ years. Jeff challenged Steve in his career, his thinking, and how he worked with people. They became great friends and business partners. We followed Jeff to three different plants in three different cities with four different companies.

We are thankful for the epicenter of what created a path for Steve to leave his corporate career to work alongside Laura. This occurred in Austin, Texas, at a Juice Plus conference in October of 2019. Amy Lewandowski, a long-time childhood friend of Laura, introduced us to Dr. Jason and Misty White from Advanced Care Chiropractic in Holly, MI. where we were introduced to Juice Plus. This led us to meeting one of our current mentors and friend, Dr. Kenny Harless, whom we met at the conference.

These friendships, relationships, business partners, and acquaintances laid the foundation for our future. Providing the opportunity to be open to new possibilities and learning to quickly change our old paradigms.

From Glory to Glory, thank you, Jesus.

NOTES

www.ingramcontent.com/pod-product-compliance
Lightning Source LLC
Chambersburg PA
CBHW060535130626
46553CB00002B/770